Shampoo

Jorge Consuegra

A darkness where even outlines are not discernible. There is a dim point of light coming from a dot on the HI-FI which is PLAYING the BEACH BOYS: "When we could say good night and still stay together... wouldn't it be niiiice?... we could be married, then we could be happy, wouldn't it be niiiiice?"
Through it there has been the SOUND of BANGING, distinct and rhythmic. It GROWS LOUDER as the MUSIC ENDS. There are also WHIMPERING SOUNDS from a woman.

FELICIA'S VOICE
Oh, no.

GEORGE'S VOICE
... what?...

FELICIA'S VOICE
That headboard.

GEORGE'S VOICE
Nobody can hear it.
It BANGS a couple of more times.

FELICIA'S VOICE
I can. It makes me nervous.
It continues to bang until Felicia screams, over the banging of the headboard. She follows the scream with a few yelps.
Silence. Now the SOUND of the PHONE RINGING.

FELICIA'S VOICE (CONT'D)
(complimentary)
Oh my God... Jesus... Jesus
Christ... Jesus H. Christ.
The PHONE CONTINUES TO RING.

FELICIA'S VOICE (CONT'D)
(a slightly different tone)
You going to answer it?

GEORGE'S VOICE
(meaning no)
Uh-uh.
It CONTINUES TO RING.

FELICIA'S VOICE
(being for her very mischievous)
Want me to?

GEORGE'S VOICE
Let it ring.
And it does. It CONTINUES TO RING, killing all other considerations.

FELICIA'S VOICE
Boy, whoever she is, she doesn't give up.
After a moment's fumbling, George finally picks it up.

GEORGE'S VOICE
Hello...
(a little surprised)
Ah, hi.
The GIRL'S VOICE on the other end of the phone can be HEARD only FITFULLY,
when George holds the receiver loosely by his ear. It is TINA.

TINA'S VOICE
What took you so long?

GEORGE'S VOICE
Wasn't sure it was you.

TINA'S VOICE
(muffled)

GEORGE'S VOICE
I... uh... I... uh... can't.

TINA'S VOICE
(laughter, sizing it up immediately)
All right, who're you with? Jill?

GEORGE'S VOICE
No.

TINA'S VOICE
(lively but muffled)

GEORGE'S VOICE
No.

TINA'S VOICE
(she's heard Felicia)
Awww --

GEORGE'S VOICE
I'll call you back.

TINA'S VOICE
Come on by.

GEORGE'S VOICE
I'll call you back...

TINA'S VOICE
(raucous laughter, muffled)

GEORGE'S VOICE
(to Tina)
Okay, okay...
He hangs up. Felicia has fished for a cigarette, lit it and coughed.

FELICIA'S VOICE
You're rude. I mean, you're very rude.

GEORGE'S VOICE
Hey, I tried to get her off the phone.

FELICIA'S VOICE
You know what I'm talking about.

GEORGE'S VOICE
No, baby. Now look, that girl that called -- I have to talk to her, she'll do something.

FELICIA'S VOICE
Like what?

GEORGE'S VOICE
I don't know, kill herself. She's O.D.'d four times.
This calms Felicia. A pause.

FELICIA'S VOICE
Well, is she your girlfriend?

GEORGE'S VOICE
No.

FELICIA'S VOICE
Are you in love with her?

GEORGE'S VOICE
Her?

FELICIA'S VOICE

Are you?

GEORGE'S VOICE
No.

FELICIA'S VOICE
Then it's not your problem.

GEORGE'S VOICE
It isn't?

FELICIA'S VOICE
No. You know too many sick ladies.

GEORGE'S VOICE
I guess so.

FELICIA'S VOICE
How do you expect to get anything done if you allow yourself to get sidetracked?
Particularly in your business... you deal with women every day...

GEORGE'S VOICE
I guess so.

FELICIA'S VOICE
Don't worry, honey, I'll protect you.

GEORGE'S VOICE
Okay.

FELICIA'S VOICE
God, I adore you.
She starts to kiss him, the SHEETS are RUSTLING. The PHONE

RINGS.
FELICIA'S VOICE (CONT'D)
Shit.

GEORGE'S VOICE
Hello.

JILL'S VOICE
You're home.

GEORGE'S VOICE
Yeah.

JILL'S VOICE
I'm coming over.

GEORGE'S VOICE
I'll call you back.

JILL'S VOICE
(firm but frightened)
No you won't.

GEORGE'S VOICE
What do you mean?

JILL'S VOICE
I told you I get 'scared up here, so if you're not coming right now...
(muffled)
I'm not kidding.

GEORGE'S VOICE
Okay.

JILL'S VOICE
(muffled)

GEORGE'S VOICE
Yeah, yeah -- 'bye.
George flips on the light.

FELICIA
Whoever she is, she doesn't give up, does she?

GEORGE
No.
Bare-assed, George swings out of bed, looking for something.

FELICIA
What're you looking for?

GEORGE
My keys.

FELICIA
I thought you said you weren't going anywhere.

GEORGE

I'm not. I mean I've gotta see this friend of mine for a few minutes.

FELICIA
You mean that girl, don't you?
George finds his keys and has begun throwing on his clothes, a pair of crumpled levis, and a brightly-colored shirt. He leaves his shorts and socks on the floor. He's obviously in a hurry.

GEORGE
What girl, she's not a girl, she's just a friend of mine.
Felicia gives him a long hard look as he dresses.

FELICIA
You son of a bitch.
George sighs, shrugs, and heads toward the door.

FELICIA (CONT'D)
Wait, at least wait 'til I'm dressed. I'm going.
She starts to get out of bed.

FELICIA (CONT'D)
Oh, Christ -- do you have any
Kleenex?
George is a little desperate now. He runs to the bathroom, tosses her the whole box.

FELICIA (CONT'D)
Thanks a lot.

GEORGE
(desperate)
Listen, baby, don't leave, really.

FELICIA
Why not?

GEORGE
I'll be right back, it's just that this girl is a different girl... she has attacks.

FELICIA
What?

GEORGE
These attacks... it's got something to do with her... uh... pancreas.
George is trying to remember the rest.

GEORGE (CONT'D)

She's got a...

FELICIA
(suddenly interested)
Does she have a pancreatic ulcer?

GEORGE
(anxious to go now)
Yeah, I think so.

FELICIA
That's very serious. Who's her doctor?

GEORGE
I don't know.

FELICIA
Gee, that's very serious...

GEORGE
I know.

FELICIA
Ruth Lesserman had a pancreatic ulcer.

GEORGE
She did?

FELICIA
It turned out to be cancer.

GEORGE
Wow.

FELICIA
So what are you doing going over there? You're not her doctor.

GEORGE
I've gotta give her some pills.
Percodan, she ran out.
Before Felicia can say anymore, George goes to the bathroom and grabs the first pill jar
he can find, moves to Felicia and kisses her.

GEORGE (CONT'D)
And listen, I'll be right back and
I want your ass in that bed when I get back.

FELICIA
(acquiescing)
You're very rude... if you don't come back --

GEORGE
I'll be back in a while.

FELICIA
I don't want to see you anymore.

GEORGE
I'll be right back, baby, really.

EXT. SUNSET STRIP - NIGHT
George on his bike threads through traffic on the Strip. OVER this, we HEAR A FEW
BARS of THE MAMAS AND THE PAPAS "Monday,
Monday." He pulls up to a signal beside a faded Eugene
McCarthy billboard. Somebody HONKS.

GIRL'S VOICE
George!

GEORGE
Hey, baby, what's happening!

GIRL
(not bad)
Nothing, my sister's back from
Vegas.

GEORGE
That's too bad.

GIRL
I have to see you.

GEORGE
Hey, stop by the shop.
He takes off. Winds through alleys and heads up the hill to
Jill's. It's a shortcut whose precision should make it obvious he's traveled it a number of
times.

EXT. AT JILL'S - NIGHT
George jumps off his bike and pounds on the door.

JILL'S VOICE
(soft)
Who is it?

GEORGE
(furious)
Who do you think it is?
JILL opens the door. She's shaking.

JILL
There were some shots.

GEORGE
What're you talking about?

JILL
Gunshots, there were some gunshots.

GEORGE
(looking around)
Where?

JILL
Here in the canyon.

GEORGE
Well, it's a big canyon.
(seeing she's upset)
Honey, I'm sorry but I've gotta get back... just for a minute.

JILL
Let me come, too.
(pleading)
Please don't leave me alone.

GEORGE
What's gonna happen?

JILL
(near tears)
I don't know... every once in a while I just get the feeling something awful's going to happen.

GEORGE
Well, like what?

JILL
I don't know... just... somebody's going to get me.
Jill starts to cry. She ambles into the carport in her nightgown.

JILL (CONT'D)
I've had these dumb dreams lately.

GEORGE
What?

JILL
They're dumb, somebody... I don't know...

GEORGE
(suspicious)
Who?

JILL
I just... who what?

GEORGE
You said somebody... who?
She's not answering.

JILL
I don't know. I can't remember. It was just in my dream.

GEORGE
No shit?
Jill laughs. George comes over to her.

GEORGE (CONT'D)
Nobody's gonna get you. Now get inside.

JILL
(uncertain)
George, I don't --

GEORGE
You'll do what I tell you. Now get the fuck inside.
She backs inside. He moves in after her.

JILL
George --

GEORGE

(moving after her)
Keep moving --

JILL
Now, George --

GEORGE
Nobody's gonna get you but me!
He leaps after her and she screams, delighted. George chases her into the bedroom. Jill screams. He throws her on the bed and leaps on top of her, kissing her. She likes it.

GEORGE (CONT'D)
How are you, baby?

JILL
Fine. How are you?

GEORGE
Great, great, fantastic. Fantastic.
Incredible. Incredible, really incredible.

JILL
What?

GEORGE
I'm gonna open the shop, baby, I'm gonna open the shop. I'm getting it together.

JILL
How?

GEORGE
(rising)
Right now -- I'm at the epitome of my life.
Right now I feel so good I'm afraid something's gonna happen.
He gets off the bed. Jill is fascinated.

GEORGE (CONT'D)
When I was a little kid, I used to want to go to Europe but right now wherever I am I'm gonna be in
Europe.

JILL
Honey, what happened?

GEORGE

I just came from a meeting... I can't talk about it now, baby. But in a few days -- see I'm disgusted with my life.

JILL
I thought you said you were at the epitome of your life.

GEORGE
I am, I am. But I've had it with chicks. They're like an occupational hazard. Six guys working for me... I'm gonna retire or settle down or something.

JILL
What about me?

GEORGE
(meaning it)
You're different.

JILL
I am?

GEORGE
You're great.

JILL
I am?

GEORGE
Yeah.

JILL
Do you really mean that?

GEORGE
Hey, baby -- I'm gonna retire with you.
He kisses her. They start rolling around on the bed.

JILL
Honey?

GEORGE
Yeah, baby.

JILL
Why am I great?
George is a little annoyed.

GEORGE
Jesus, I don't know. You're great.
Jill looks a little perplexed.

JILL
Will we live together?

GEORGE
We live together now.

JILL
But in the same house, you know, one house.

GEORGE
(just a slight hitch)
-- Sure.
She hugs him.

INT. JILL'S BEDROOM - LATER
George in bed, beginning to sleep. Hubert Humphrey expresses opinion at his chances
tomorrow on TV.

JILL
Maybe you don't even like children.

GEORGE
Of course I like children.

JILL
You've never even been around one.

GEORGE
I'm around you and I like you, don't I?

JILL
(smiling despite herself)
Yeah.

GEORGE
Okay...
(sinking back down)
Night, baby.

JILL
(after a moment)
George?

GEORGE
What!

JILL
Not right now, I don't mean right now... but eventually...

GEORGE
(grumpy)
Okay, baby. Okay...

JILL
Jackie says she wouldn't bring children into this world. That it's hypocritical and overpopulated.

EXT. BANK OF AMERICA - DAY
A FEW BARS OF THE BEATLES AND "SGT. PEPPER" OVER George on bike whipping into bank parking lot.

INT. BANK OF AMERICA - DAY
George sits talking, with MR. PETTIS, a bank vice president.
He is perspiring a little. Somebody's breathing rather heavily. It's Mr. Pettis seated behind his desk now and opposite George. He's going over something.

PETTIS
(looking up now)
Oh yes. Mrs. Shumann called about you.

GEORGE
(smiling)
Right.

PETTIS
How is she?

GEORGE
Great.

PETTIS
Wonderful woman.

GEORGE
She is.

PETTIS
I went to school with her husband.

GEORGE
Great.

PETTIS
(pleasantly affirmative)
So you want to go in business for yourself?

GEORGE
Right.

PETTIS
And you need money?

GEORGE
Right, that's right.

PETTIS
(smiling)
You do know what money's like these days.

GEORGE
(no)
Well, yeah... you know.
Pettis grabs a sheet off his desk, one in plastic containing rates.

PETTIS
Jesus, look at this. Nine, nine and three quarters -- that's our prime rate. And I'll tell you something else: the big boys are going for it.

GEORGE
They are?

PETTIS
After all, Mr. Roundy, we're paying six percent. Six percent. FHA's at eight and a half -- no, we won't be going back to the old days.

GEORGE
I guess not...

PETTIS
It's got nothing to do with inflation. Rates, for example, rise independently of tight money if you look at interest curves carefully.
Historically, that's always been true, though most people don't realize it.
An uncomfortable pause.

PETTIS (CONT'D)
What sort of references do you have?

GEORGE
Well, I do Barbara Rush.

PETTIS
Pardon me?

GEORGE
(embarrassed now)
Her hair, I do Barbara Rush.

PETTIS
I mean credit references, Mr.
Roundy.

EXT. MELROSE COFFEE HOUSE - DAY
Jill Haynes and JACKIE SHAWN, in mini skirts and boots, are having coffee at one of
the interior decorator hangouts outdoors off Melrose in West Hollywood.
A CAR HONKS. A Cadillac pulls up to the curb. Its occupant
HONKS again, obviously trying to attract their attention.
Jill starts to look over.

JACKIE
I think you're crazy. Don't look over, it's Lenny Silverman.

JILL
Who is that?

JACKIE
(deadly)
A real swinger. He's been trying to fuck me for about two hundred years.
LEONARD is now calling Jackie's name. Jackie can't avoid it anymore.

JACKIE (CONT'D)
(pleasantly)
Hi, Leonard.

LEONARD
Jackie, what're you doing?

JACKIE
(they're having coffee)
Going for a pony ride at
Kiddielands, want to come along?

LEONARD
I have to meet a client... who're you dating?
Jackie looks off and spots a billboard.

JACKIE
Poster-Kleiser.

LEONARD
Oh yeah?

JACKIE
That's right.

LEONARD
I'll call you.

JACKIE
Fine.

LEONARD
See you later.

JACKIE
Anyway, you're crazy.

JILL
I am? I mean why?

JACKIE
Oh, honey, don't be totally naive.

JILL
I'm not. Maybe I am.

JACKIE
No, listen. He's a very good hairdresser.
Jill looks at Jackie.

JACKIE (CONT'D)
Well, he is.

JILL
(annoyed)
So what's your point?

JACKIE
Jill, I'm just trying to be helpful.

JILL
I know, I'm sorry.

JACKIE
I spent three years with him. I just couldn't take it not knowing who was gonna pay the rent... his unemployment or mine. George was adorable but it drove me crackers.
Now at least I'm comfortable.
Lester does what he says he'll do.
Maybe you're happy living like a gypsy. Are you?

JILL
George is great but I know what you mean.

JACKIE
Face it, you can go around with cute guys and get hung up on their sexy bodies and things like that but sooner or later you've got to find somebody. Face it, time isn't on your side.

JILL
I guess not.

INT. BANK OF AMERICA - DAY
George and Mr. Pettis.

GEORGE
(giving it all he's got)
I've got the customers... that's my point. I'm the one they want. If I had my own shop, they'd leave and come to me. I have a lot of customers.

PETTIS
Look, Mr. Roundy, why don't you make out a financial statement?
It'll save us both some time. Miss
Michaels here can show you... have it notarized and we'll see where we go from there.
Miss Michaels, would you get me a couple of forms?
Pettis rises, shakes George's hand and disappears. George is left with MISS MICHAELS, who has been more or less within earshot of the whole conversation. George is very upset.

INT. OFFICE WAITING ROOM - DAY
Jill thumbs through a Life magazine with Eldridge Cleaver on the cover, waiting for an interview in the outer office of the 9000 Building whose open window overlooks a smoggy chunk of the city.

She's one of so many girls that at first she's not recognizable. All of them have composites which they carry in leather folders. They eye each other uneasily.

INT. INTERVIEW OFFICE - DAY
There is the PRODUCER, Barry, and the director, JOHNNY POPE.

JILL
Egypt?

POPE
That's right.

JILL
But why Egypt?

POPE
Well, that's where the pyramids are and we want real pyramids in the ad.
Jill nods.

PRODUCER
You seem disappointed.

JILL
No... how long did you say?

PRODUCER
Three weeks.
Jill nods.

JILL
Egypt?
Pope, chagrined, shoots Jill a look. He's trying to get her the job.

PRODUCER
Look, is there somewhere else you'd rather go? Maybe we can change our location.

JILL
No, it's not that...

PRODUCER
Do you have children?

JILL
No.

PRODUCER

Are you married?

JILL
No.

PRODUCER
Do you have something against traveling?

JILL
(unable to interpret
Pope's looks to her)
No.

POPE
Well, do you have something against us?
Jill laughs, a little embarrassed.

JILL
No!

PRODUCER
(to Pope, he's wasting time)
John...

POPE
(ignoring him)
Go ahead, Jill, you can say it.

JILL
Now I'm embarrassed to tell you.
She is, too, and Pope can see it.

PRODUCER
We'll let you know tomorrow.

JILL
Please don't misunderstand... I'd really like to go.

PRODUCER
(a little sarcastic)
Thanks for coming by.
Jill is at the door. She turns back. To Pope.

JILL
Oh. thank you.

POPE
Sure.
Jill leaves.

POPE (CONT'D)
(shaking his head)
This town...
At the shop on Brighton Way in Beverly Hills. A FEW BARS OF
SIMON AND GARFUNKEL'S "SOUNDS OF SILENCE" covers George pulling up
on his bike.
The street is empty of traffic except there are scores and scores of parked cars, a few
parking lot attendants, and some meter maids. George starts toward the shop. A pair of
women in colored smocks and huge curlers burst out of the shop.
They look like Medusas. They hurtle down the sidewalk as if they're running from
something.
Then they find their respective cars and begin pouring pennies into the meters. CLINK,
BUZZ, CLINK, BUZZ.
George looks glum. He's walking along the street. A GIRL stops him. She's driving by
in a 3.4 Jag.

GIRL
Hi, George.

GEORGE
Hey, baby, what's happening?

GIRL
Nothing, I reconciled with Ron, you know, the guy I divorced last summer.

GEORGE
Great, great. I hope you make it.
Somebody HONKS in back of her.

GIRL
Call me!

GEORGE
I don't have your number, stop by the shop.

GIRL
(waving goodbye)
Okay!
George looks after her, smiling. Then:

GEORGE
(disgusted)

God damn it.
He goes into the shop.
A large gilt mirror on one wall of the shop. It covers most of the wall it leans against.
An attractive young woman in her early thirties, everything matching, a real French
garden, leans forward INTO SHOT and looks at herself in the mirror. She studies her
image carefully. She moves closer to it. She seems uncertain at first. Then as she looks
her conviction grows:

TINA
Great... great... great... great... great!
She turns back to DENNIS LOLLY, her hairdresser. She takes his hand.

TINA (CONT'D)
Great, Dennis.
With her other hand she touches her hair.

TINA (CONT'D)
Do you think there's enough height?
I mean do you think there's enough height?
Now she and Dennis look into the mirror at her together.
Dennis toys with the calico scarf around his neck. Felicia, in far corner, waits defiantly.
George spots her.

TINA (CONT'D)
George, do you think there's enough height?

GEORGE
(on way to Felicia)
Yeah, sure.

TINA
Dennis doesn't think so.

DENNIS
Man, I didn't say a word.

TINA
Well, what do you think? Is there enough height?
Both Dennis and Tina turn back to the mirror for further deliberation.

FELICIA
You're late, George.

GEORGE
(taking her to his cubicle)
I gotta talk to you.

FELICIA
I don't want to talk about it...

GEORGE
But you don't know what happened.

FELICIA
I don't care.

TINA
George, do you think there's too much height?

GEORGE
(seating her)
It's great. You don't know what happened, this girl she almost got--

FELICIA
(a little hysterical)
I don't care about that girl, I don't care if she's dead.

GEORGE
Calm down, baby.

FELICIA
(calming down)
I'm perfectly calm, George, I'm simply saying you have no respect for me, that you're incapable of distinguishing between me and one of your average Hollywood... mummers...

GEORGE
-- What?

FELICIA
Nummers.

GEORGE
What?

FELICIA
-- Numbers, and I don't need to place myself in that kind of position.
GLORIA tugs on George's arm.

GEORGE
What're you here for?

GLORIA
(as if giving away a secret)
-- A wash and set.

GEORGE
No.

GLORIA
No?

GEORGE
You need a cut.

GLORIA
But Mr. Norman said --

GEORGE
Said what!

GLORIA
(whispered)
I just needed a wash and set, a wash and set, that's all.

GEORGE
Well, baby, I'm George and it needs to be cut.
(to Felicia)
But I don't want to place you in that position either.

FELICIA
-- I like myself far too much, far too much.

GEORGE
I don't want to place you in any position --

FELICIA
-- to be put in that kind of position...

GEORGE
(to Gloria)
I'll have Mary wash you. Mary!

MARY
(a schvar)
Yeah!

GEORGE

Wash her.

MARY
(looking at Gloria)
What with?

GEORGE
(nudging her)
-- A brillo pad, I don't care, anything.
Mary has gone over to the shampoo stand above which are several photographs of models and one of a handsome young black Marine in fatigues. George has gone to pick up a razor, changes it.

MARY
-- You takin' a lot of shit lately,
George.

GEORGE
-- Oh yeah.

MARY
(mixing)
But then again you ask for it -- you just like my Otis -- can't keep his hands outta ladies' hair either.
George laughs.

GEORGE
-- White ladies?

MARY
(laughing, too)
-- Oh my yes.

FELICIA
(burning with anger)
George --

GEORGE
(calling back)
I'm coming, baby --
(to Mary)
How's Otis doing, anyway?

MARY
That boy always does great. He's a corporal or a squad leader or something, just wrote me from some place called Kwang Due?

GEORGE
I don't know if you don't know --

FELICIA
George!
George winks at Mary, heads back.

FELICIA (CONT'D)
(going right on)
I'm not used to that kind of treatment.

GEORGE
What kind of treatment?

FELICIA
(going right on)
I've never been treated that way, and I'm not going to start now.

GEORGE
Jesus, I don't know, baby, I been cutting too much hair lately. I'm losing all my concepts...
Jill has entered the shop. She approaches George.

JILL
George.

GEORGE
Hey, baby, what's happening?

JILL
They want me to go to Egypt for three weeks.

GEORGE
Great.
Jill stands there now, not knowing what to say.

GEORGE (CONT'D)
Jill, say hello to Felicia.

JILL
Hello.

FELICIA
Hello.

JILL
George.

GEORGE
Yeah, baby...

JILL
How did it go at the bank?
George looks away.

GEORGE
Great.

JILL
Could I talk to you for a second?

GEORGE
Hey, I'm, you know --

JILL
Could I?
George moves away from Felicia.

GEORGE
Yeah.

JILL
(with some feeling)
I said I wasn't sure if I could go.

GEORGE
Go where?

JILL
(impatiently)
Egypt!

GEORGE
Oh, great, listen, baby, I gotta get back, okay?

JILL
Okay, but how did it go at the bank?

GEORGE
Great... can we talk later?

NORMAN
(the shop's owner)
George!

GEORGE
Yeah.

NORMAN
You're late, we're all backed up and you're supposed to go to
Buffums.

GEORGE
Buffums?

NORMAN
Yes, Buffums.

GEORGE
I've got heads here, Norman.

NORMAN
You promised you'd do the show.

GEORGE
Oh fuck, Norman!

NORMAN
Don't use that tone of voice with me... never mind, I'll take Gordon.
George turns back to Felicia as RICCI comes by. He's near tears.

RICCI
Do you know what that Lillian
Bercovici just did?

GEORGE
(working on Felicia)
No, man.

RICCI
-- Right after I sprayed her?

GEORGE
What?

RICCI
(losing control)

She touched it! Then she played in it and got it all into something else. Now I don't know what it is!

He's waiting for George for sympathy. Jill steps away gathering patience.

RICCI (CONT'D)
I can't even stand to talk to her on the phone.

GEORGE
(sympathetic)
She's heavy.
(to Felicia)
See, Norman expects me to get in here, take care of all the customers and then do his show out in Norwalk. I gotta have my own shop, just out of self defense.

FELICIA
I can see that.

GEORGE
You're looking great, baby.

FELICIA
What're you doing later?

GEORGE
(half kidding)
Whatever you say.

FELICIA
We have this political thing tonight. Could you comb me out at the house?
George is torn.

GEORGE
I don't know. I'm beginning to feel guilty.

FELICIA
What about?

GEORGE
All I ever do is play. I should be doing something to get my own shop open.

FELICIA
Why don't you see Lester?

GEORGE
(a little alarmed)
Your husband?

FELICIA
Yes.

GEORGE
(not sure what she's driving at)
What about?

FELICIA
The shop. I think you're a good investment, and I don't mind telling him.

GEORGE
Hey, listen, baby, I'm a star.
Jill returns.

JILL
George.

GEORGE
Hey, baby, say hello to Felicia.

JILL
I already said hello.

GEORGE
Okay.

JILL
George.

GEORGE
Yeah, baby.

JILL
When can I talk to you?

GEORGE
Baby, I'm in the middle of work.

JILL
I know but this is important. I have to make a decision.

GEORGE
About what?

JILL

Whether or not I'm going.

GEORGE
Going where?

JILL
Egypt.

GEORGE
Honey, have they offered you the job?

JILL
No, but I think they might.

GEORGE
(to Jill)
Just a second, I'll be right with you...
He turns back to Felicia. Jill moves away.

FELICIA
(interested)
Is she all right?

GEORGE
I don't know. Just a minute...
George moves over to Jill.

GEORGE (CONT'D)
What do you want?

JILL
Your advice!

GEORGE
They didn't offer you the job yet.

JILL
I want your feelings about it.

GEORGE
Right now?

JILL
Look, either we have a meaningful relationship or we don't, I've got to know.

GEORGE

(really harassed)
Look, baby, can we talk about it later?
Felicia is watching them.

JILL
When?

GEORGE
When I get off work.

JILL
When is that?

GEORGE
I'll call you.

JILL
When is that, George?

GEORGE
I'll call you.

JILL
(really upset)
But I never know when you're working and when you're not working!

GEORGE
(half to himself)
Neither do I, baby.

JILL
What?

GEORGE
Nothing, I'll call you, okay?

JILL
... Okay...
Back to Felicia. As Jill leaves.

GEORGE
-- Anyway.

FELICIA
I hope she's all right.

GEORGE
She's fine. You really think I'd be a good investment?

FELICIA
I wouldn't say so if I didn't.

GEORGE
No, I know.

FELICIA
And I certainly wouldn't tell
Lester.

GEORGE
I know.

FELICIA
I mean it or I wouldn't say it.

GEORGE
That's great. You look great, baby, great. Dennis, look at Felicia's hair.
Dennis stops. He's with the DESK GIRL. Both of them:

DENNIS & DESK GIRL
Great.

EXT. SHOP - DAY
Jill, in street, on verge of tears... moves to her car... gets in... sits for a long moment.

EXT. OFFICE BUILDING - DAY
George on bike pulls into office building. The MUSIC OVER is

JEFFERSON AIRPLANE'S "WHITE RABBIT."
INT. LESTER'S OFFICE - DAY
In his inner office.
LESTER'S on the telephone, staring out the window.

LESTER
Look, Kurt, I don't care where you have to go. I want Beluga Caviar there. Call
Jurgenson's, call
Chasen's... I don't care how much it costs... how much?... then spend it. Just make sure
it's there.
You've got all the money in the world to buy it. You understand?
Just make sure it's there on the table tonight.
(he hangs up)
Jesus.

(to George, to no one)
You've got to do everything yourself. You know?
Suddenly Lester gives George a steely look. It covers his hair, his clothes. George is
acutely uncomfortable.

LESTER (CONT'D)
Felicia says you're a very good hairdresser.

GEORGE
Well, yeah.

LESTER
She says you're a fabulous hairdresser.

GEORGE
Thank you.

LESTER
I didn't say it, she did. How'd you happen to get in that line of work?
George sort of knows what Lester's driving at.

GEORGE
Oh, well, I went to beauty school... you know you go to beauty school... and you get
your operator's license... and you graduate... and you're a hairdresser.

LESTER
I see.
Long pause. George hasn't told Lester what he wants to know.

LESTER (CONT'D)
It's an unusual trade.

GEORGE
Yes it is.
An awkward pause.

LESTER
But the important thing is you're successful at it.

GEORGE
In a way. But...

LESTER
But what?

GEORGE

I'm better than the guy I work for.
This seems to interest Lester.

LESTER
Well, George, I invest for a lot of people. I make a lot of money for them. More than
they could do for themselves.

GEORGE
After a while that hurts... doesn't it?
Lester smiles. He appreciates this.

LESTER
It's good you want to do something,
George.

GEORGE
Thank you.

LESTER
But personal services are not the kind of thing I usually get into.

GEORGE
They're not?

LESTER
(suddenly direct, almost enthusiastic)
No, they're a pain in the ass, there's no way of keeping track of anything. It's a cash
business and you've got to watch your operators or they'll steal you blind, am I right or
am I right?

GEORGE
You're right.

LESTER
Who needs that kind of aggravation?
Who needs that kind of aggravation at my age? When I finish work I want to...
The door bursts open. It's one of the SECRETARIES.

SECRETARY
Mr. Karpf...
Jackie is right behind her. She bounces in, not seeing
George.

JACKIE
I'm sorry but I need an extra garage key.

In Lester's presence she seems distinctly younger than she did with Jill. She's startled
when she sees George.

LESTER
What for? What do you need the key for?
Jackie continues to stare at George.

JACKIE
The man from Sloan's is coming. I called you about it.

LESTER
How did you lose that key? Oh,
George, this is uh Miss -- this is
Jackie.

JACKIE
Oh, hi, I mean hello, we've met.

LESTER
(a little suspiciously)
Is that right?

JACKIE
(almost immediately on the defensive)
Well, yes, George is a wonderful hairdresser.

LESTER
Is that right?
Awkward pause.

JACKIE
So how's Norman?

GEORGE
Great. Who's been doing your hair?
Jackie glances at Lester.

JACKIE
I go to the blue'n gold barber shop in Westwood. The guy in the third chair's dynamite...
nobody much.

LESTER
George is going to open a shop.

JACKIE
(really interested)

No kidding? Your own shop?
George starts to say yes.

LESTER
George, could you -- excuse us for a minute?

GEORGE
Sure.
He leaves the office, shuts the door, leaving Jackie and
Lester alone. Lester shuts the door.

LESTER
I called to tell you I was sending one over but the line was busy, you're always on the
phone.

JACKIE
I am?

LESTER
Who were you talking to?

JACKIE
Who do you think I was talking to?

LESTER
My secretary saw you with that boy.

JACKIE
Steve?

LESTER
Whatever his name is, that actor.
Jackie looks for a moment as if she's going to get very emotional.

JACKIE
Steve Slutes, and he's not a boy.
(a touch bitter)
Steve couldn't get arrested as an actor. He couldn't get arrested as a boy.

LESTER
Then you were talking to him.

JACKIE
I ran into him at the 76 station on little Santa Monica, what was I supposed to do, hide
in the ladies room? Yes, I was talking to him.
Lester's a little chagrined now but not much.

JACKIE (CONT'D)
(an outburst)
I'm always on the phone because you never let me see anybody, I can't even bring my girlfriends over to the house because they might run into you. You're driving me up the wall, Lester. You're even jealous of the dogs. I mean I've gotta have somebody I can talk to.

LESTER
I'm not jealous of the dogs.
Jackie looks at him in disgust.

LESTER (CONT'D)
(very positive)
Now listen, Jackie, I'm not jealous of anybody, I just can't afford to get caught... off base.

JACKIE
So I can't talk to some broken down actor, what do you think, I'm going to tell him I'm screwing Lester
Karpf!

LESTER
Of course not.

JACKIE
That's not very logical, Lester.

INT. OFFICE - GEORGE AND SECRETARY picking up the tail end of this.

SECRETARY
He thinks the room is soundproofed.
Don't tell him it's not.

GEORGE
How come?

SECRETARY
He'll have that awful construction crew back again, and they can never do anything right.

INT. LESTER'S OFFICE
LESTER
(trying to think of why)
It's very logical, it's the most logical thing in the world. You wouldn't feel this confined if we could go out with people and have dinner, and a little conversation and so forth...

JACKIE
Really? How about starting with tonight?
By her tone, Jackie indicates she's been saying all of this for months. Lester repeating it like it's just occurred to him genuinely upsets her. She's near tears and she's not the kind of girl who cries easily. Lester's sensitive to it.

LESTER
Sweetheart, I know it's rough but at this point -- my business involves handling money for some very touchy people, politics and so on... Felicia's at a very difficult period in her life... any divorce and settlement and so forth, my finances would have to be looked into.
Jackie knows what he's talking about.

JACKIE
(quietly)
You and your touchy investors.

LESTER
(finally)
Look... you do well for people, they don't ask you to stop. Nobody wants you to stop making money, doll, not even Uncle Sam. They all want their share.
Jackie comes over to Lester.

JACKIE
You're lying about one thing,
Lester.

LESTER
What's that?

JACKIE
You're still jealous.
She's said it provocatively and like the younger girl she can be with him. Lester smiles. He's almost benign.

LESTER
God, you're a doll.
He takes her in his arms and she responds.

LESTER (CONT'D)
(he means it)
We'll work something out about tonight, I promise...

INT. OFFICE - GEORGE AND SECRETARY
The door opens. Jackie and Lester emerge, distinctly subdued.

LESTER
Angie, give Miss Shawn a garage key for the Bowmont House, would you?

ANGIE
Yes, Mr. Karpf.
Angie opens her desk and goes through some files, pulls out a key, puts it in an envelope and hands it to Jackie -- she's lightning quick about it, super efficient.

LESTER
Well, let's go down together.
C'mon, George, I'll walk you out.

LESTER, JACKIE AND GEORGE IN HALLWAY BY ELEVATOR
Jackie turns to stub out a cigarette in a standing ashtray.

LESTER (CONT'D)
(quietly)
Felicia's really interested in the shop, isn't she?

GEORGE
Oh yeah.
Jackie moves back.

LESTER
(normal tone now)
Well, George, you may not think ten or fifteen grand means much to me, but I invest for myself and a lot of particular people.

GEORGE
Oh yeah? I mean I know.

LESTER
So I'm going to want a little more of your thinking on the subject.
The elevator doors open.

GEORGE
When?

LESTER
When?
The doors close on the three of them.

INT. ELEVATOR going down. George is looking at Lester, waiting for an answer.

LESTER

(looks up slowly)
How about tonight?
Jackie looks to Lester. Lester winks at Jackie.

GEORGE
Tonight?

LESTER
Yeah, little election party I'm giving at the Bistro.
It's a pain in the ass but -- I have to do it. We'll have a little time to talk there.
The elevator stops on the third floor. A man in a suit and a middle-aged woman with a cane get in. They're strangers to each other. The elevator proceeds.

LESTER (CONT'D)
(quiet, almost solemn in their presence)
-- maybe you could, on your way, you know, pick up Jackie here.

GEORGE
(slowly)
Okay.
They've reached the basement and are standing as Bill the maintenance man, races around the cars to get to Lester's
Rolls.

LESTER
It's good you want to do something,
George.
George doesn't answer this time.

LESTER (CONT'D)
I wish my son knew what he wanted to do.

GEORGE
Oh yeah?

LESTER
-- Anything, I don't care what it is, just so it's something.

GEORGE
I know what you mean.
Lester's car is backed up. The door opened for him.

LESTER
(thoughtfully)
Maybe he ought to go to beauty school. Anyway, see you tonight, doll, okay?

JACKIE
Fine.
Lester slips Bill a few dollars and takes off, leaving Jackie and George looking at each other. Jackie shakes her head.

JACKIE (CONT'D)
Jesus...

GEORGE
-- Yeah... your car down here?
Jackie nods. They walk toward it.

GEORGE (CONT'D)
-- Listen, I'm supposed to take
Jill to El Cholo tonight. She's really going to be pissed if I don't.

JACKIE
-- Maybe she'll come with us. If I tell her how important it is to me,
I don't think she'll mind. Do you?

GEORGE
I don't know. Probably not.

JACKIE
Jill's really great, isn't she?

GEORGE
Great... so how's everything with you?
They've reached Jackie's 230SL.

JACKIE
Great, more or less.
She starts to get in.

GEORGE
How long you had this?

JACKIE
Oh, about six weeks now... Lester -- well, he's very sweet.

GEORGE
I'm sure.

JACKIE
He's a very private person, actually.

GEORGE
Yeah -- he doesn't happen to know that we went together, does he?
Jackie has started to get in the car several times. This stops her again.

JACKIE
-- Well no. It never came up.

GEORGE
You going to tell him?

JACKIE
(smoothly)
-- What for? Honey, I'll see you later.
They kiss each other's cheeks, she gets in and takes off.

EXT. SANTA MONICA BOULEVARD - JILL AND JACKIE - DAY tooling along
the tracks in Jackie's 230SL.

JACKIE
Jill, you're a real sweetie pie.
You really are.
(she glances over at Jill)
You're sure you don't mind?

JILL
Don't be silly.

JACKIE
You're really a love -- you sure?

JILL
-- No. No really.

JACKIE
Well, what is it, honey?

JILL
Nothing.

JACKIE
It must be something.

JILL
Well, it's George.

JACKIE

I thought you said things were great with George.

JILL
Well they are. But we have problems. You say things are great with Lester. Is he going
to marry you?

JACKIE
We don't think marriage is important.

JILL
But you have problems?

JACKIE
-- Yeah, honey...

JILL AND JACKIE
JILL
I don't know. One minute he's up in the air and makes love to me five times a day and
tells me everything's going to be great and he's getting his own shop and then suddenly
he disappears and he won't even talk to me. It's driving me crazy.
Jackie pulls away from the signal a little jerkily.

JACKIE
Five times a day?

JILL
(sighs, then)
-- I guess it's all got to do with this shop.

JACKIE
Really, Jill, aren't you exaggerating just a little? Five times a day?

JILL
(embarrassed)
Well, you know what I mean.

JACKIE
After four years? No I don't... and
I don't know too many girls who do.

JILL
I'm exaggerating.

JACKIE
How much?

JILL
(giggling a little)
Jackie --

JACKIE
What?

JACKIE AND JILL
JILL
(taking a little breath)
Well... it's not so much the number of times he does it, it's... he does it for a long time.

JACKIE
He does?

JILL
Well yes -- you know that about
George.

JACKIE
It's been so long I don't how long?

JILL
Quite a while... an hour, an hour and a half -- sometimes forty-five minutes -- that's quite a while, isn't It?

JACKIE
I would say so, yes.

JILL
Honey?

JACKIE
What?

JILL
I think you're going to hit that car in front of us.
Jackie slams on the brakes.

INT. UNEMPLOYMENT LINE - JILL AND JACKIE - DAY standing there.

JILL
-- See, I just know that if I go to
Egypt, well, things happen, I just don't know what'll happen to us, he just never seems to think ahead, does he?

JACKIE
-- When you say forty-five minutes or an hour, do you mean continuous time? Just continually, without stopping?

JILL
-- Well -- not going in and out, I don't mean just that. Why are you asking me? You went with George longer than I have.

JACKIE
-- I guess I just blocked it out, that's all.

JILL
C'mon.

JACKIE
Well, there was this one time --

JILL
(a little devilish)
-- Yesss?

JACKIE
-- I was in the kitchen doing the dishes and George was out in Long Beach doing a show...

JILL
(meaning yes)
-- uhh-huhh...

JACKIE
-- Well it was very hot so I'd left the door open and the water was running so I didn't hear him come down the stairs...

JILL
... Mmm-hmmm.
Now Jackie has begun to lose her self-consciousness and is into the story. A little faint edge of nervousness or something like it begins to take over Jill.

JACKIE
-- He came up behind me and I was wiping a dish and he just... lifted up my skirt, and, you know, right there...

JILL
Didn't you have any panties on?

JACKIE

(remembering)
-- He reached up and tore them.

JILL
What did you do?

JACKIE
Well... I just kept wiping that dish. Maybe it doesn't sound very sexy but it was.

JILL
(faintly perturbed)
No, it sounds very sexy -- did you just stay by the sink all that time?

JACKIE
No, he picked me up and carried me out to the sundeck -- God, it was hot. The wood on the sundeck, everything.

EXT. LESTER'S HOUSE - BEL AIR - AFTERNOON
A gardener is riding a mower around the front lawn. There are three cars parked in and around the circular driveway.

INT. BEDROOM - LESTER
He slips into a cardigan sweater. His vanity is restricted entirely to how well pressed and clean everything is he wears.
He goes out of the dressing room toward the kitchen, passing
Lorna on the phone in the living room and Felicia at dining room table, hair in curlers, reading Cosmopolitan magazine.

LESTER
Do you think George is a fairy?

FELICIA
Who?

LESTER
That kid... the hairdresser.

FELICIA
Well, I don't know for sure... he's a hairdresser.
Mona brings her coffee from kitchen.

FELICIA (CONT'D)
Thank you, Mona.
Lester has swallowed some vitamins in the kitchen. Turns to her.

LESTER

Maybe he's just a kooky guy who likes doing something kooky like that.

FELICIA
Maybe... why do you ask?

LESTER
I'm thinking of investing with him.
He worries me.

FELICIA
Why?

LESTER
Maybe he's too flighty and irresponsible. That's why I asked if he was a fairy.

FELICIA
I don't know. He's a hairdresser.

LESTER
(really asking)
You suggested it, don't you think it's a good idea?

FELICIA
Yes, but... I thought...

LESTER
What?

FELICIA
That you were just indulging me.

LESTER
No, doll, I listen to you. And if a deal loses money that's not so bad either if it's handled right.
He gives Felicia a peck and starts out.

LESTER (CONT'D)
He's a nice boy. I invited him tonight. I'm sorry he's a fairy.

INT. SHOP - GEORGE AT WORK - DAY
George is busy. He's working on ANJANETTE.

ANJANETTE
You're in a good mood today,
George.

GEORGE
Yeah, baby. Things are great.
Listen, there's Devra, whatta you want?

ANJANETTE
Chicken salad.

GEORGE
Chicken salad, Devra!

DEVRA
I don't have any change.

GEORGE
Get some at the desk.

ANJANETTE
Anyway, you remember Harold?

GEORGE
Yeah, baby, how's it going?
The PHONE RINGS. Norman brings it to George.

NORMAN
George... Jackie Shawn.
George seems really surprised to hear the voice on the other end. Anjanette looks around.

GEORGE
No, I'd like to but I've got too many heads here, can't you stop by the shop?
(to shampoo girl)
Two caps, Mary, yeah, two.
(back to phone)
Okay, but I have to be in Bel Air at four...
He hangs up. It RINGS again.

ANJANETTE
Don't you think there's too much gold?

GEORGE
(to Anjanette)
It's great.
(into phone)
You wanna speak to Mary? Hold on...

ANJANETTE

I don't know, I think...

GEORGE
(good natured, but firm)
Look, would you argue with your doctor?

ANJANETTE
No.
Ricci comes up to him ready to cry.

GEORGE
(to Ricci)
Hey, what's happening?
(calling)
Mary! Telephone.
(to Ricci)
What's the matter?

RICCI
(furious)
Wanda...

GEORGE
Oh yeah?

RICCI
You were supposed to handle that bitch, she's always asking for you, and she was furious you weren't here.

GEORGE
Yeah?...

RICCI
She's murdered her hair... you do something with her, I'm never going to touch her again.

GEORGE
I'm busy, man.

RICCI
If I have to touch her again, I'll throw up!

GEORGE
(exploding)
Don't talk like a child. You're a pro, now get out there and cut!

Ricci is stunned. He says under his breath, "I'll throw up" again and leaves. Mary, her back to George, sits holding the telephone to her ear.

ANJANETTE
I thought you were in a good mood.

GEORGE
I am... except I've gotta do somebody at their house.

ANJANETTE
Don't you like her?

GEORGE
No, it's a very groovy girl.

ANJANETTE
Then what's the problem?

GEORGE
(really worried)
She's a very groovy girl. That's the problem.

ANJANETTE
What're you talking about, George?

GEORGE
Well, it's a small town. Sooner or later things catch up with you... don't they?
Mary runs out of the shop, tipping over a magazine rack.

GEORGE (CONT'D)
Where's the caps, Mary?
She's exiting front door in a hurry.

GEORGE (CONT'D)
Mary? What's goin' on, Mary?

EXT. GEORGE ON HIS MOTORCYCLE - MOVING - DAY
MUSIC, THE BYRDS, "TURN, TURN, TURN."
He pulls up to a rustic house. He gets his little case off the bike and then hesitates. He walks to the door and rings the bell.
Jackie answers the door. She seems distracted and, at the same time, a little wary. Much the same, in fact, as George.

JACKIE
Hi. C'mon in.
Jackie's wearing a robe. They walk into the living room, the dogs yelping.

JACKIE (CONT'D)
Shut up, it's all right.
(to George, automatically)
Do you want a drink?

GEORGE
No, thanks.

JACKIE
Well, I do.
She starts to mix herself a drink. She changes her mind, pours herself a shot of whiskey and hurls it back. She does it again. When she turns back to George he's looking at her noncommittally.

JACKIE (CONT'D)
Where do you want to do this?

GEORGE
Probably the bathroom.

JACKIE
Can't you do it out here?
George looks around.

GEORGE
Well, it depends. If you just wanted a combout. I guess I could.
Jackie turns to him, honestly uncertain.

JACKIE
Well, what do you think?
George himself is tentative.

GEORGE
I don't know. Why don't you sit down.
Jackie looks around a little at a loss and finally sits down on the glass-topped coffee table.

JACKIE
(meaning her position)
Is this all right?
George moves in. He draws the drapes back so light comes in from the backyard and the swimming pool can be seen.

GEORGE
Yeah.

He takes her hair in his hands. The contact makes them both nervous. She looks away.
George continues to run his hands through her hair.

JACKIE
(a little nervous)
Well, what do you think?

GEORGE
I'd cut it...

JACKIE
You would?

GEORGE
Yeah, I think so...

JACKIE
(almost irritable)
You don't seem very sure.

GEORGE
No, I'm sure.
There is a moment where Jackie is trying to decide whether she'll let George actually
cut her hair.

JACKIE
(then)
Okay... but I want you to know one thing.
(almost a threat)
I've got to look great tonight, I mean I have to look great, okay?

GEORGE
Okay.

INT. FELICIA'S BEDROOM AND DRESSING ROOM - DAY
Felicia is throwing on a bandana and wraparound sunglasses.
She seems in a hurry.
She leaves the bathroom, moves quickly through the house to the kitchen. She passes
Lorna's bedroom. LORNA is changing from her school clothes into a tennis dress. She
watches her mother flash by.

IN THE KITCHEN
Felicia stops. She is holding a dangling pearl earring in her hand.

FELICIA
Mona, Mona!

MONA comes out from the laundry room. Felicia has called a little too loud.

FELICIA (CONT'D)
(indicates earring)
Have you seen the other one of these by any chance? I want to wear them tonight.
(before Mona can answer)
Oh... when George gets here, tell him to wait. I have to pick up a dress and I may have
to have it fitted, but be sure...
Lorna ambles into the kitchen, expressionless.

FELICIA (CONT'D)
... to tell him to wait.

MONA
Yes, ma'am. But I have to go to the market...

FELICIA
Just be sure he doesn't leave.
Felicia flashes out the door and into the carport, visible through the kitchen. She takes
off. Lorna slowly slips a white swetlet onto her slender wrist.

INT. JACKIE'S BEDROOM AND BATH - DAY which includes a sauna. Jackie's
got on a terry-cloth robe.
George has been wetting her hair in the basin. Her terry cloth robe is bulky and
obviously in the way.

JACKIE
Jill's coming with us.

GEORGE
Great.

JACKIE
She's incredible...
(after a moment)
She loves you, George.

GEORGE
Yeah... I mean great.
George begins to cut. Jackie winces a little. George notices it.

JACKIE
Getting my hair cut is always a little nerve-wracking.
The cutting goes on. The bathroom is very close. George has begun to perspire a little
as has Jackie.

JACKIE (CONT'D)
... I don't get it done often.

GEORGE
Whew.

JACKIE
What's wrong?

GEORGE
It's hot in here.

JACKIE
(after a moment)
It's the sauna, I keep the sauna on and it makes the whole bathroom hot.

GEORGE
Yeah... wow.
George stops and takes off his shirt. He's wearing a purple T shirt underneath. He goes back to cutting. Jackie's getting more and more edgy, partly because of George's proximity and partly because of her concern over what he's doing. George on the other hand is now less tentative, more focused on the job at hand.

JACKIE
(finally)
Not too much, don't cut too much.

GEORGE
Jackie, would you argue with your doctor.

JACKIE
The shrink? Many times.
George stops and looks at her. Both are perspiring freely now.

JACKIE (CONT'D)
Bernstein... seemed to think I hated men.

GEORGE
Do you? You still see him?
Jackie tries to look at her hair in the mirror. George gently pulls her back.

JACKIE
(with some feeling)
No.

GEORGE

Why not?
Jackie doesn't answer.

GEORGE (CONT'D)
Why not?

JACKIE
... he tried to... uh... make it with me.

GEORGE
And?

JACKIE
And what?

GEORGE
Did you?
Jackie looks up slowly. George is still cutting, not looking directly at her.

JACKIE
It was after you, baby. After you.

GEORGE
(breathes deeply)
Boy, that sauna is really... can't you turn it down or something?

JACKIE
No... Lester likes it on all the time in case he wants to use it.

INT. JILL'S BEDROOM - DAY
Jill, alone, sits on bed. Gazes into bureau mirror, shaping her hair. The PHONE RINGS.

JILL
Hello... oh hi, Johnny. Oh really?
Thank you... Are you serious?...
Tonight I'm busy, I... Right now?
Oh no, you really couldn't come up here.

INT. JACKIE'S BEDROOM & BATH - DAY with Jackie's hair considerably shorter.
George is sitting now as he works, his knee wedged between her legs, working very
close.

JACKIE
Anyway, he offered me a silver cloud. At least he should give me a
Ferrari and pay off my house and give me a nine carat ring or something...

GEORGE
(amused)
Did Lester know about him?

JACKIE
There was nothing to know.
Anyway... if I can't have love I have to at least have money. I have to have some pride
I can do something.
George has started to dry her hair. He stops. He picks up the scissors. Her hair is askew
still so it's difficult to see what George has done.

JACKIE (CONT'D)
(staring at the scissors, a warning)
George...

GEORGE
I just have to do one little thing.

JACKIE
If you screw me up for tonight,
I'll kill you, I swear to God, I'll kill you.

GEORGE
I won't screw you up.

EXT. SUNSET BOULEVARD - LESTER DRIVING - DAY his dark blue Rolls
Royce. He's listening to the radio, keeps switching to pick up fresh news reports.
He turns off Sunset and heads up Coldwater Canyon.

INT. JACKIE'S BATH AND BEDROOM - JACKIE AND GEORGE - DAY
JACKIE
George... how about Felicia?

GEORGE
(expressionless)
What?

JACKIE
Did you?

GEORGE
Did I what?

JACKIE
You know what I'm talking about.

GEORGE
Hey, I don't tell.

JACKIE
(teasing)
Can I count on that? I just want to see Lester with me and that cunt in the same room
tonight.

GEORGE
Yeah?

JACKIE
Well, did you or didn't you?
George shuts the blower off. He picks up his comb for the final comb out.

GEORGE
Now, baby... if I told you about her... then you couldn't count on me not telling
anymore... could you?

JACKIE
You did, didn't you?
They're very close and Jackie's moving closer. She's intrigued, amused and at ease.
George is trying to keep some distance.

GEORGE
Baby...

JACKIE
You did, I know you did.

GEORGE
One of my few virtues is discretion.

JACKIE
You just can't stand to miss one of them, can you?
She's moving closer and closer, being deliberately provocative -- to seduce the
information out of him.

EXT. JACKIE'S STREET - DAY
Lester pulls into it. He stops, reaches in the glove compartment and pulls out one of the
little airline bottles of vodka. He pours it into a glass, drinks it. He notices
George's bike in the driveway. Next to him on the seat is a prettily wrapped package.

INT. JACKIE'S BEDROOM AND BATH - JACKIE AND GEORGE - DAY

George sprays her. He turns her around in the chair to face the mirror so she can see
herself for the first time. She should look really different, her hair significantly shorter,
and modishly and beautifully cut to her face.
Jackie's lips part.

JACKIE
(softly)
George...

GEORGE
(staring at her)
Yeah, baby...

JACKIE
You're a genius.
Her hand automatically goes up to take his. He starts to pull it back.

JACKIE (CONT'D)
(grabbing it, thrilled)
You're a genius, do you know that, you're a genius?
She turns and throws her arms around George, kissing him.
It's too much for George. He kisses her back.

JACKIE (CONT'D)
(trying to resist)
Oh, no.
George is obsessed. He wraps his arms around her and she responds, passionately.

JACKIE (CONT'D)
Oh, no.
They are grappling, pushing and pulling with each other.
George kicks away the stool by the mirror and tries to bend
Jackie to the rug-covered bathroom floor.

JACKIE (CONT'D)
(genuine)
No! Don't! Please!

GEORGE
(forcing her down)
I don't want to... I swear...
She throws her arms around him, kissing him and shoving him away. George is tearing
at his trousers. They are on the floor now , rolling around, bouncing gently off the
ceramic molding from the sunken tub.

JACKIE

It'll ruin everything.

GEORGE
I know... you don't know, I know.

JACKIE
Don't, don't, don't...
They hit the sauna room door as they're rolling around and the door opens. Steam comes pouring over them, momentarily obscuring their struggles. George has trouble getting his pants down. At the last instant, Jackie gives them a helpful tug.

JACKIE (CONT'D)
(moans)
Oh, no...
Suddenly, the DOGS begin to BARK. There is the SOUND of the DOOR OPENING. Jackie sits up.

JACKIE (CONT'D)
It's Lester.
She's frozen with fear.

LESTER'S VOICE
(muffled)
Hey, doll... Jackie... honey... where are you?

JACKIE
Get up, get up, get up.
George is already trying to pull on his trousers. Jackie is up and clutching her robe, unable to move.

JACKIE (CONT'D)
Oh God, oh God, oh God... do something, please God, do something.

LESTER'S VOICE
(nearer)
Hey, baby, are you sleeping?

GEORGE
Sit down.

JACKIE
(frantic)
What are you talking about?

GEORGE
(equally frantic, forcing her)

Sit down!

WITH LESTER
He's moved into the bedroom, carrying the package obviously a gift for Jackie. He's been a little puzzled. His puzzlement is rapidly turning to suspicion.

LESTER
Jackie?... Jackie?
Lester opens the door. He's hit with a blast of steam and the sight of George stripped to the waist, ostensibly working over Jackie who is loosely wrapped with a towel. George has a comb in one hand and now turns on the dryer, blowing it with a somewhat exaggerated gesture.

JACKIE
Shut the door, shut the door!

LESTER
Oh, I'm sorry.
He shuts the door. Then he thinks better of it. He opens the door again and takes a step into the bathroom.
George waves the comb at Lester a little impatiently. It's wet and sprinkles Lester.

GEORGE
Look, either come in or stay out!

JACKIE
Shut the door, Lester. What do you think this is, a picnic?

LESTER
(confused now)
Sorry, honey, I...

GEORGE
That's okay, that's okay, just shut the door.
Lester shuts the door, feeling a little chagrined, and relieved. He sits on the bed and puts the present beside him.
In a moment George emerges.

GEORGE (CONT'D)
... she's very upset...

LESTER
What about, tonight?

GEORGE
(seizing the opportunity)

That, and... I'll be done in a minute.
He goes back inside.

IN THE BATHROOM GEORGE AND JACKIE just stare silently into mirror at each other.

LESTER'S VOICE
Jackie?... Hey, I brought you a little something, doll.

AT THE DOOR - LESTER AND GEORGE
George has his case of comb and scissors, etc., and is standing with Lester. He's anxious to go.

LESTER
You look like you've had quite a work-out.

GEORGE
It's nerve wracking sometimes... women can get you very upset.

LESTER
I know it, I know it.

GEORGE
... this doing hair it's...

LESTER
I know it, son. But tonight's going to be even tougher.
George just looks at him. Lester walks him to bike.

LESTER (CONT'D)
George, I know you have to deal with Felicia and you're caught in the middle, and if you can just bear with me tonight, well, I appreciate the way you've handled the situation.

GEORGE
Oh, hey...

LESTER
It's a difficult situation, and I want you to know I appreciate it.
Tonight's going to be real tough for me --

GEORGE
I don't know what to...

LESTER
Son, we'll do business, I can tell you that.

George roars off on bike.

JACKIE AND LESTER IN KITCHEN
Jackie is cleaning up some dog food. Lester stands there for a minute.

LESTER (CONT'D)
I'd like a drink.

JACKIE
(looking up)
Just a second, I've gotta clean this mess up or the dogs'll have it all over the house.

LESTER
You ought to get rid of those dogs.
Jackie looks up and then controls herself.

LESTER (CONT'D)
They get hair all over the place.

JACKIE
They're Yorkies and they don't shed.
Jackie goes into the living room and fixes Lester a drink.
Lester follows.

JACKIE (CONT'D)
(giving him a drink)
Here.

LESTER
Aren't you going to have one?

JACKIE
No.

LESTER
Why not?

JACKIE
Because I don't want one.
Lester goes over to her to kiss her.

LESTER
C'mon, doll, it's five o'clock, have a drink.
Jackie turns away and explodes.

JACKIE

I don't want one! First you tell me not to drink then you tell me to drink, which is it? I don't want a drink!

Lester's now a little intimidated, but even more suspicious.

LESTER
I called to tell you I was on my way, but the line was busy, you're always on the phone.

EXT. LESTER'S HOUSE IN BEL AIR - DAY
George pulls into the circular driveway. COVERED by a few bars of The Mama's and The Papa's "California Dreamin."

There's only one car.

George gets off the bike and goes to the door. Nobody answers. He hears the SOUND of a BALL BANGING. He looks toward the tennis court.

ON THE COURT - LORNA is banging away on the backboard. There's a basket of balls nearby. She hits with considerable skill and power until she misses the backboard and the ball lodges in the steel mesh surrounding the court.

George is standing there. Lorna looks at him.

LORNA
You here to see my mother?

GEORGE
Yeah.

LORNA
She's out, but you're supposed to wait.

LORNA WALKING TO GEORGE
LORNA (CONT'D)
Hungry?

GEORGE
A little.

AT THE KITCHEN TABLE
They're eating silently. Lorna has hauled all kinds of food out of the refrigerators. She watches George as he eats with some relish. She gets up and goes to the steel-doored refrigerators.

LORNA
(indicating refrigerators)
This is the one thing I like about this house... want some lox?

GEORGE
No thanks.

LORNA
You're my mother's hairdresser?

GEORGE
(warily)
I do her hair, yeah.

LORNA
Chopped liver?

GEORGE
No thanks.

LORNA
Are you gay?... baked apple?... they're cold but they're good.

GEORGE
No thanks.

LORNA
Did you hear me?

GEORGE
Yeah.

LORNA
Well, are you? Are you queer?

GEORGE
... yeah.

LORNA
(laughing)
C'mon, are you or aren't you?

GEORGE
(trying to avoid it)
Gee, this is great.
He slices a piece of cheesecake. Lorna sits down, in the chair nearest him now.

LORNA
C'mon, tell me. Don't be afraid.

GEORGE
Why do you wanna know so bad?

LORNA
See if you've been making it with my mother.

GEORGE
(looking at her for a minute, he changes his tone)
What would my being a faggot have to do with that?
Lorna shrugs.

LORNA
Nothing, I guess... have you ever made it with a guy?

GEORGE
Have you ever made it with a girl?

LORNA
I asked you first.

GEORGE
Yeah... I've made it with a girl...
Lorna smiles. A pause.

LORNA
Well, are you?

GEORGE
Am I what?

LORNA
Making it with my mother?
George wants to avoid this at all costs. He stares at Lorna intently.

GEORGE
I'd like to do your hair sometime.

LORNA
Why?

GEORGE
... just, you could look very heavy...

LORNA
Don't make conversation with me.

GEORGE
What?

LORNA
You don't have to make conversation with me, I'm not my mother... do you have a thing
about older women... that's sort of faggoty isn't it?
George is weary and getting annoyed.

GEORGE
Yeah, it is.

LORNA
I never get my hair done.

GEORGE
No kidding.

LORNA
In fact, I don't think I've ever been to a beauty parlor in my whole life.

GEORGE
No shit.

LORNA
You think that's funny, don't you?

GEORGE
(laughing a little)
Yeah.

LORNA
You live a phony cheap cop-out existence.

GEORGE
(determined to be light)
Yeah...

LORNA
Beverly Hills hairdresser... what kind of a thing is that to do... you might as well be a
faggot... think that's funny too?

GEORGE
No.

LORNA
Then what do you think?

GEORGE

That you're just like your mother.

LORNA
I am not like my mother!

GEORGE
You are.

LORNA
I am not!

GEORGE
You are.
Lorna is furious.

LORNA
I am not!

GEORGE
(he starts to placate her)
Look...
(then defiantly)
Do you wanna fuck me?

LORNA
(defiantly)
Yeah.
George stops eating. He's not prepared for this.

GEORGE
(uneasily)
Right now?

LORNA
(a little more tentative now that the moment has arrived)
Yeah.

EXT. SOURCE RESTAURANT - JOHNNY POPE AND JILL - DAY
A scraggly bearded WAITER with long stringy hair sets down two huge green salads before Jill and Johnny Pope.
In so doing the Waiter drops a wooden menu he's been carrying. As he bends down to pick it up, he kneels beside
Pope. Pope taps him on the shoulder.

POPE
(tapping him)

Oh, scraves...

WAITER
Yes?
The Waiter looks up, and moves.

POPE
Thank you.

WAITER
What for?

POPE
Taking your hair out of my salad.

WAITER
Oh, I'm sorry.
Pope nods, Jill giggles. The Waiter goes off. Pope tosses out a few pieces of lettuce from the top of his salad.

JILL
Why don't you ask for another one?

POPE
Are you kidding? His hair's probably the most nutritious thing in here. See, you've reduced me to eating weeds.

JILL
... my friend doesn't like it here either.

POPE
All right, forget this filth.
Continue about your friend.

JILL
Well he's not exactly a friend.

POPE
Is he an enemy?

JILL
(laughing)
Of course not... he's sort of a boyfriend.

POPE
-- sort of a boyfriend?

JILL
Sort of.

POPE
I see. You mean he just sort of fucks you.

JILL
Johnny!

POPE
My God, did I say that? I don't believe it.
He looks under his chair to see if it was somebody else.

POPE (CONT'D)
I'm terribly sorry.

JILL
(amused)
-- never mind.

POPE
What does he do? Is he an actor?

JILL
-- no.

POPE
Good for you.

JILL
He's a hairdresser.
Pope drops his fork in the salad bowl.

POPE
-- oh, sure. A hairdresser. How... how do you a... meet a hairdresser?

JILL
Getting your hair done...
(looks at him, abruptly)
Would you like to go to a party?

POPE
Not with your hairdresser.

EXT. LESTER'S HOUSE - FELICIA - DAY pulls into the driveway. She gets out of her car, spots
George's bike.

INT. THE KITCHEN
She sees the food spread out.

FELICIA moving through the house. She stops by Lorna's room. Lorna has a sliding door, which is closed. Felicia opens it.

FELICIA
Lorna?

LORNA'S BEDROOM
Lorna is sitting on her bed, in her tennis dress but with her tennis shoes off. She's straightening a string in her racket.
She looks to her mother, expressionless.

FELICIA (CONT'D)
Have you seen George?

LORNA
He's in the bathroom.

FELICIA
Your bathroom?

LORNA
Yes.
The toilet flushes. The sink runs, and George emerges. He's looking a little haggard.

GEORGE
Hi.

FELICIA
(coolly)
Hello, George.
They walk out to the lanai together and George picks up his case. There is considerable tension from Felicia as they walk into her bedroom. Felicia slides the bedroom door shut, an action which George unhappily notices. She turns to George.
She looks very hostile. She's trembling.

FELICIA (CONT'D)
I've missed you.
George is taken aback. He gropes for a moment.

GEORGE
I've... missed you too.
Felicia comes to him. She comes to him and touches his arm.
George suddenly flings his case across the room and pounds his fist into a high-backed chair, turning away from Felicia.
She clearly misunderstands the action.

FELICIA
(touched)
It's okay, honey... it's okay now.
She moves to the door and quietly locks it. George winces.
She comes back to him and kisses him gently. She kisses him again with more passion. George tries to respond.

FELICIA (CONT'D)
Comb my hair out later, honey.

GEORGE
No, that's okay, I'll do It now.

FELICIA
No, baby... I'm glad you're coming tonight.
She gently tugs at him, leading him toward the bed. George is miserable.

GEORGE
(looking toward the door)
But aren't you...

FELICIA
Right now, I just don't care.
As they sink to the bed, Felicia switches on the HI-FI. The Tijuana Brass begin to play.

GEORGE ON HIS BIKE - LATE AFTERNOON
COVERED BY a few bars of Bob Dylan's "Like a Rolling Stone".
Riding home. He turns down his street and pulls into his driveway. He gets off his bike and only as he starts up his walk does he see Jill. She's been quietly waiting on his front porch, hidden in the shadows of the overhang. She doesn't look happy. George stops cold.

GEORGE
(?)
Jill says nothing.

GEORGE (CONT'D)
Where's your car?

JILL
A friend dropped me off.

GEORGE
Who?

JILL
Never mind. Where've you been?

GEORGE
A business meeting, I told you that.
They go inside. The living room is messy. George looks around in disgust.

JILL
What business meeting?

GEORGE
Look at the way I live.

JILL
I've been trying to reach you all afternoon. You weren't in the shop.
What is this thing tonight?

GEORGE
What do you mean, what is it? It's some political bullshit.

JILL
I have to have Jackie ask me? Don't you think you could call me and let me know? Look
at my hair.

GEORGE
Wait a minute, God-damn-it. Do you think I want to go to some God damned party? I'm
trying to get that God damned shop open. I'm trying to get a little bread together. That's
all I'm doing.
George's outburst has shocked Jill. George maniacally begins straightening the mess.

GEORGE (CONT'D)
I just wanna live like everybody else, that's all. I want clothes in the closet, and food in
the refrigerator, and I don't want shit all over the house and running my ass all over
town... I want my own house... I want an appointment book... I want to get up in the
morning and go to bed at night... I want a normal life like everybody else, that's all.
He collapses into a chair. She comes over to him and knee beside him.

JILL
I know, honey.

GEORGE
Maybe I should get a dog... no, it would just shit all over the house and I'd never clean it up.

JILL
(laughing a little, touching him)
Oh, honey. If we had one place, we could have a nicer place and I could take care of it. We're almost never here.

REAR VIEW MIRROR - NIGHT
A signal red Porsche cabriolet pulls up into mirror. The top is down. Under the brightly lit streetlights Jill's blonde hair and features are VISIBLE.

WITH GEORGE AND JACKIE in her Mercedes. George still looking through the rear view mirror. Jackie's a knockout.

JACKIE
(looking at George looking in mirror)
-- you'll be the prettiest thing in the room -- light's green...

GEORGE
(he takes off)
-- oh yeah... what do you know about this guy?

JACKIE
-- what guy?

GEORGE
(gesturing toward rear window)
-- this guy with Jill.

JACKIE
He's a director.

OUTSIDE OF BISTRO - GEORGE AND JOHNNY POPE - NIGHT pull up, Pope right behind George. Parking ATTENDANTS leap for the doors.
A few photographers of the movie freak variety ask each other who these arrivals are. One assures several others that they're nobody.

GEORGE
(to Attendant)
Do I need a ticket for this?

ATTENDANT
We'll remember you.

POPE as they move to take his Porsche.

POPE (CONT'D)
(shaking his head)
I'll park it.
Pope drives his own car onto the lot.

WITH JILL, GEORGE AND JACKIE waiting for Pope who is now ambling toward them.

GEORGE
(to Jill)
What does he direct besides traffic?

JILL
Ha, ha.

GEORGE
Television or movies?

JILL
Commercials.

JACKIE
(quietly, to George)
Feel better? Let's go.
Pope has joined them.

INT. BISTRO FOYER
They clear it to see the long elegant bar, bathed in soft light, filled with elegant customers.
George looks and sees someone. A fortyish WOMAN, attractive.

GEORGE
(to Jackie)
Jesus Christ, there's Norma Stern.
Look at her hair.

JACKIE
What about it?

GEORGE
Looks like somebody took a dump in it, that's the worst color job I've

--

Norma comes over, hugs George.

NORMA
George --

GEORGE
(pointing to her hair)
Baby, you've been chippying on me --

NORMA
Yes, isn't it awful --

GEORGE
(smiling)
-- yes.
Jackie tugs him by the arm.

JACKIE
We're upstairs, George. Now come on. Behave yourself, and for
Christ's sake, do me a favor. Don't let me drink too much.

GEORGE
(going upstairs)
You don't do that anymore, do you?

BISTRO STAIRS
Jackie doesn't answer. They've reached the top of the stairs.
They're hit by the full force of the upstairs gathering -- black tie, posters of Nixon,
Agnew, Reagan, and Murphy, vaguely familiar faces crossing back and forth,
clustering, watching early returns on television sets that are blaring from various points
around the room. An ORCHESTRA PLAYS Meyer
Davis Society Jazz. Jackie and George hesitate. Pope and Jill are behind them. Pope
jostles George as he stops, abruptly.
George looks around. Pope smiles. He's holding Jill's hand.
George notices. Jill disengages her hand casually, as though it were necessary only for
the walk up the stairs. Jackie nudges George, forcing him to move into the room with
her as
Lester comes toward them. He's stopped on his way over.

WAITER
Can I get you folks something?

JILL
A stinger, please.

POPE

A tomato juice.

GEORGE
I'll take a -- some white wine.

WAITER
And you, madam?

JACKIE
(searching the room)
Oh I'll uhh -- just a coke.
The Waiter moves on and they wait for their drinks.
Lester finally makes to them.

LESTER
George, glad you could make it, son. Hi, doll.

JACKIE
Lester, this is my friend Jill and this is Johnny Pope.

LESTER
Glad to meet you, Jill, Mr. Pope.

INT. BISTRO UPSTAIRS
George turns to get his drink from the Waiter as do Jill and
Pope. Lester takes Jackie's arm.

LESTER
Who are they?

JACKIE
(quickly)
Jill Haynes, Jill Haynes, I've told you about Jill a hundred times,
Lester, you never remember anything
I say.

LESTER
Does she know about us?

JACKIE
Jesus, she's my best friend.

LESTER
Who's the guy, George's boyfriend?

JACKIE

I don't know. Why don't you ask him?

LESTER
C'mon, Jackie, I'm only trying --
George --
He draws George aside.

LESTER (CONT'D)
-- do me a favor, kind of keep your eye on Jackie, she's a little high strung tonight --

GEORGE
-- yeah?

LESTER
See she doesn't drink too much.
Jackie has heard this last. Lester turns to her.

LESTER (CONT'D)
See you later, doll.
Jackie puts down her coke, picks up a glass of white wine from a passing tray and downs it in one gulp, putting it on another tray and picking up another glass of white wine.

FELICIA with cleavage carefully prominent in a strapless gown, spots
George. She excuses herself from the couple she has been talking with and goes straight to the powder room.

INT. POWDER ROOM - FELICIA checks herself out in the mirror, glossing her lips with a pale tint of something or other. She gives a final anxious look, then hurries out, nearly bumping into a lady coming In.

OUTSIDE she moves through the crowd up behind George, turning him around.

FELICIA
George, darling.
She kisses him full on the lips, lingering on it.

GEORGE
(without batting an eye)
Hey, baby, what's happening. Oh this is Jackie. Jackie, say hello to Felicia.
It is only now that Felicia sees one of George's arms has been holding onto Jackie.

JACKIE
(also without batting an eye)
Hello, Felicia.

FELICIA

(instantly suspicious of
George)
... hello.
Felicia looks from George to Jackie and back again.

FELICIA (CONT'D)
I'm so glad you could make it. I've been looking forward to seeing you.

LESTER pours his drink on the cuff of a distinguished MAN sitting beneath him at a table as he sees George and Felicia and
Jackie clustered together.

WITH LESTER AND MAN
MAN
Lester, what the fuck do you think you're doing?

LESTER
Jesus, Nate, I'm sorry.
Lester fumbles, tries to clean Nate off with a napkin.

NATE
Never mind, I'll do it myself.
He dips the napkin into a glass of ice water and proceeds to clean off his cuff.
Nate goes back to the TV monitor where Agnew is making some remarks or commentators are repeating his comment about being a household word.

LESTER
So far so good.

NATE
Aw there's nothing to worry about.

LESTER
You never know.

FELICIA WITH GEORGE
FELICIA
Why didn't you come alone? Lester invited you. Did you have to bring her?

GEORGE
(looking toward Lester)
Well she...

FELICIA
She what?

GEORGE
She's a friend of Jill's.

FELICIA
And who's Jill?
She spots Jill.

GEORGE
Well, she's a friend of Johnny
Pope's -- you know, the director.
She looks at Pope who is saying something to Jill which is making her laugh.

FELICIA
Oh.

GEORGE is threading his way through a crowd, holding two drinks, one of them a coca-cola. It's a little more raucous now, with election returns from the television sets creating a more festive mood. Now and then someone jumps up from a set and hugs someone so carrying drinks is a little dodgy.

JACKIE, F.G. - LESTER, B.G., TALKING
Jackie sits alone by the bar, an unlit cigarette in her mouth. A man offers her a match. She stares at the burning match as if it's obscene. She blows it out.

JACKIE
No thanks.
The man looks a little shocked, moves on.

GEORGE has his arm held. It's KENNETH, a red-haired decorator.

KENNETH
Excuse me, I know I know you, but I can't think where.

GEORGE
Look, I'd like to help but --
Felicia grabs George's other arm pulling him away from
Kenneth. Kenneth looks a little shocked at the ferocity of
Felicia's move.

FELICIA
There you are.
She tugs him with her.

GEORGE
Wait a minute --
She takes him right into the ladies room, George still juggling the drinks.

JOHNNY POPE watches Felicia and George disappear into the ladies room, looking over Jill's shoulder. Jill has not seen it.

POPE
This other couple that we're here with, do you know them very well?

JILL
Well... sure...

POPE
Then maybe you can tell me why
George would be going into the ladies room.
Jill looks around and stares at the door.

JILL
George? Was he alone?

POPE
I don't think so.

JILL
Well did he go in there with
Jackie?
Pope points over to Jackie sitting at the bar drinking now.

JILL (CONT'D)
That bastard.

POPE
George is a hairdresser, isn't he?
Jill doesn't answer.

INT. BATHROOM - FELICIA AND GEORGE
GEORGE
(desperate)
Baby, you gotta let me out of here.
Felicia kisses him.

FELICIA
Sweetheart, it's a bore out there... let's lock the door.

GEORGE
Holy Christ. You want to get us killed?

FELICIA

Don't be silly. I'll just tell
Lester we were smoking a couple of joints. See?
She pulls two joints out of her beaded bag.

LESTER only a few seats from Jackie, Jackie staring daggers at him,
Lester aware of it. He's talking to a pair of lacquered eminence grises.

LESTER
-- fellas, fellas, just listen, you both have tidelands, you both want
Uncle Sam to come through with offshore drilling permits -- so do it together --

JACKIE has taken an olive from an olive tray and hit Lester on the back of the head.
He's finished this little dissertation. He sees the source of the missile. He grows pale,
frozen.
Sixty-four year old bejeweled WOMAN in b.g.

WOMAN
So, little red riding hood says 'my what big teeth you have and the wolf says all the
better to eat you with, my dear, and she says -- eat, eat, eat, doesn't anybody ever fuck
any more?'
Jackie has now picked up a carrot from a relish tray. George appears.

GEORGE
Don't do it.

JACKIE
That son of a bitch, everything he says is a phony piece of shit, what does he think, I'm
some cigar butt he's got between his teeth --

GEORGE
(almost picking her up)
C'mon, cunt, you're going for a walk.
He takes her into the next room and Lester watches the move with a mixture of relief
and concern.

INT. OTHER BAR
Jackie is now near tears.

JACKIE
He just completely ignores me. He could have at least said something, introduced me
or something.

INT. SMALL BAR
GEORGE
Sweetheart, you're drunk.
She leans on George.

JACKIE
Oh God, what do I want, George?
Lester comes hurrying in, sweating, now.

LESTER
Hi, doll, what's wrong?

JACKIE
You know what's wrong.
Felicia trips coming into the small bar.

FELICIA
Lester --
Lester straightens up like he's been shot.

LESTER
Oh, Felicia, there you are, you know George and uh -- uh --
He's genuinely forgotten her name.

JACKIE
Jackie Shawn.

LESTER
Yes, Jackie Shawn, my wi --
Felicia.

FELICIA
We've met.

JACKIE
Yes.

GEORGE
Well anyway...

LESTER
(to Felicia)
Your hair looks -- well fabulous.

FELICIA
That's George.

INT. SMALL BAR
LESTER
It's just -- fabulous.

(to George, an attempt at levity)
Think you could do anything for me?

GEORGE
(he takes it seriously)
Well -- I could try. Do you wash your hair every day?

LESTER
Isn't that bad for it?

GEORGE
No it keeps the skin peeling.
You've got to keep the follicles open. You lose hair and the skin grows over the follicle and that's how you lose it.
George actually touches Lester's hair, professional interest growing.

GEORGE (CONT'D)
This really ought to be layered...

LESTER
Layered?

GEORGE
Well yeah, otherwise it just sort, you know, lies there -- layer so it kind of fluffs out --
He starts to fluff Lester's hair a little when Johnny Pope walks in with Jill to this. Pope stares at them.

POPE
I think they're waiting for somebody to start dinner.

LESTER
Have they sat down?

POPE
Everybody but us.

FELICIA
They're waiting for you, Lester.

INT. BISTRO DINNER TABLE
Dinner is pretty much finished, waiters have begun picking up plates.

IZZY SOKOLOFF
(to Jill)
I guess it's almost impossible to get work in the business these days.
Pope watches Sokoloff make his move.

JILL
Well, commercials. I read for a soap the other day.

IZZY
A soap?

JILL
A daytime soap opera.

IZZY
And?

JILL
I was too old.

IZZY
What was it, somebody's daughter?

JILL
Somebody's mother.

JACKIE'S PLATE is untouched. She holds up her wine glass.

JACKIE
Waiter!
George looks at her.

JACKIE (CONT'D)
One word out of you and I'll gargle with it.
The waiter pours the wine. George looks to Jill, shrugs. Jill mouthes, 'try and stop her.'
George mouthes back, 'are you kidding?'

INT. BISTRO
SID ROTH has been eyeing Jackie.

SID ROTH
Aren't you hungry, Miss Shawn?
Jackie looks at Roth. Roth shoots his cuffs and smiles.

JACKIE
Not for rubber chicken, no.
Sid Roth smiles. Jackie smiles back.

SID ROTH
(intime)

Well maybe I can get you something.

JACKIE
That's very sweet of you, Mr. Roth.

SID ROTH
Sid.

JACKIE
Sid. You must be a very important executive.

SID ROTH
(almost a whisper)
Well, whatever I am, I think I can get you whatever you'd like.

JACKIE
You do?

SID ROTH
Yes.

JACKIE
(same tone as Sid's)
-- well, more than anything else --
(indicating George)
-- I'd like to suck his cock.
She points to George. George chokes on the last of a piece of chicken. Sid Roth is stunned. He doesn't know what to do.
George is coughing badly. Jackie slaps his back.

HEAD TABLE - FELICIA AND LESTER
Felicia is listening to Lester. The Agnew and Nixon posters are directly behind them.

LESTER
(to East)
-- Senator, you should've seen those little kids! About forty of
'em, all blind. We put out these mattresses on the front lawn and they came running out of the house, tripping and falling all over the place, having a hell of a good time. I mean they were blind of course. But it really gave you a feeling of accomplishment. I tell you I never had such a good time.
Felicia during the above has looked up to see Jackie fawning over George. She can't believe her eyes.

FELICIA
Lester --

SENATOR
-- let me understand this was exclusively a home for blind children --

FELICIA
Lester --

LESTER
-- yes, Senator -- just a minute, dear --

FELICIA
Lester, don't you think that uhh --
Now Lester spots it. He's very confused.

FELICIA (CONT'D)
That girl's making an awful spectacle of herself.

LESTER
(angry himself)
What do you expect me to do about it?

FELICIA
I just thought you'd like to know --

LESTER
Why would I like to know if there's nothing I can do about it, goddammit --

OTHER VOICE
Quiet! Cranston's on.
They quiet down.

JACKIE AND GEORGE
Jackie's now moving around kissing George on the mouth.
Jill is watching. Johnny Pope is fascinated.

JILL
-- Jackie really shouldn't drink --

POPE
-- oh I don't know --

JACKIE
(arm around George's shoulders tonguing his ear)
-- Just get me out of here, baby. I can't stand it. It's killing me.

GEORGE
(indicating head table)

-- we can't now.

JACKIE
-- why not? C'mon, take me out of here, somewhere I don't have to lie to anybody and I'll fuck your brains out, you little fiend, I adore you --

FELICIA is watching Jackie and George with ever greater intensity, her mouth growing more and more agape.

JACKIE AND GEORGE
JACKIE (CONT'D)
(plaintive)
-- don't you want to --

GEORGE
Jackie, can we --

JACKIE
(a little louder)
Who's the greatest cocksucker in the world? C'mon --
George looks around sweating now.

GEORGE
(very quietly)
-- you are.

JACKIE
Fuckin' A --
With that she slips right under the table. It's a surprisingly fluid move.

FELICIA almost simultaneously rises, knocking her chair back.

LESTER sees both moves and interrupts the Senator.

LESTER (CONT'D)
Senator, excuse me a moment --
He turns to Felicia and then looks over toward Jackie's empty chair and literally doesn't know which way to go first. He's a little like the bear in the penny arcade that is shot and keeps turning one way, then another. Finally he heads toward
Jackie's vacant chair and George.

GEORGE his chin to the tablecloth is fishing under it for Jackie.

GEORGE (CONT'D)
Now, Jackie --

JILL
(trying for aplomb)
-- she's a very compulsive girl.

POPE
I can see that.
Lester rushes up.

LESTER
(a desperate smile)
Hello, George. Your friend feeling a little under the weather?
Jackie surfaces through the tablecloth.

JACKIE
(to Lester)
-- you phony asshole --

LESTER
(as if he didn't hear it)
Oh, dear that's too bad.
(with quiet desperation, to George)
-- get her out of here, get her out of here.
A cheer goes up as some late returns come in. Dirksen is talking about a new mandate for law and order and peace with honor.

LESTER (CONT'D)
(to Sid)
What was that?

SID ROTH
Illinois.

LESTER
(doesn't know what he's saying)
-- oh, good.

INT. BISTRO
Lester glances back toward Felicia who is watching him.

GEORGE
Jackie, c'mon --
George moves to Jill.

GEORGE (CONT'D)
I've got to get her out of here.

JILL
-- go ahead.

GEORGE
-- well aren't you --

JILL
-- what?
(indicating Pope)
-- I'll see you later...

GEORGE
(not liking it too much)
-- okay --
(pointed)
-- I'll see you later. Your house.
He moves away with Jackie. Lester turns back toward the main table.

INT. 230SL - JACKIE AND GEORGE - NIGHT driving down Sunset Boulevard.
There is a long moment of silence. The RADIO'S PLAYING the Eve of Destruction.
George gives Jackie a couple of sidelong glances.

JACKIE
(finally)
-- gee...

GEORGE
-- what?

JACKIE
(she sits up, lights a cigarette)
I don't know what gets into me.

GEORGE
You were great.

JACKIE
No, I blew it, I blew it with
Lester.

GEORGE
No you didn't.

JACKIE
You don't think so? I do.

GEORGE
You were great.

JACKIE
You always say that... I really care for Lester, don't I?
George laughs.

GEORGE
That sounds like me.

JACKIE
I am you, you little bastard.
She starts to scrunch over and kiss him, then stops.

JACKIE(CONT'D)
Where do you want to go?

GEORGE
Sammy's?

JACKIE
He still having parties?

GEORGE
He never stopped.

INT. BISTRO - FELICIA IS SITTING WITH LESTER fuming. A woman, ROSALIND, is painstakingly and painfully introducing the Senator.

ROSALIND
... and so... to have this man... here... among us... who has helped... as has everyone here to bring so many people together... of all races, creeds, and colors...

FELICIA AND LESTER
Rosalind droning on, b.g. She finally introduces Senator
East.

INT. BISTRO - FELICIA AND LESTER
FELICIA
Lester.

LESTER
Yes, sweetheart, shh.
He pats her hand. She gives him a look that could kill.

FELICIA

-- I hope you like Miss Shawn --

LESTER
-- what, who? Oh she's very nice, yes -- I mean normally ---

FELICIA
-- cause she's going to be very, very expensive.

LESTER
Can't we go into this later, sweetheart?

ROSALIND'S VOICE
Ladies and gentlemen, to Senator
Joe East.
Glasses are raised, a little dissonant hurrah.

FELICIA
We cannot go into this later.

LESTER
That's okay too.

FELICIA
You make me sick. Just be straight for once in your life.
There are now O.S. calls for East to do his Indian chant.

QUICK CUT TO:
EAST
SENATOR
-- this tells of the ancient grandmother who, upon seeing the garden gate of her childhood, stops a moment and says, hello garden gate, hello garden gate, garden gate, hello.

INT. BISTRO - LESTER AND FELICIA
LESTER
(finally exasperated)
-- look, Felicia, this party involves more than you and me, you know. These people are concerned about more than each other, you know.

FELICIA
-- is that right?

LESTER
-- yes, we're all trying to do something to make this a better country to live in, believe it or not.

THE SENATOR has begun his weird chant, beating out accompaniment on a cigar box and a pewter vase.

FELICIA
(glancing up)
-- is that what this is all about?

LESTER
Yes and you don't have to be sarcastic about it, that's a beautiful thing he's doing -- some people do more than go to the beauty parlor and shop at Saks --

FELICIA
Lester, you're a miserable man.
You're not helping anybody. You're just twisting arms to raise money for a lot of silly son of a bitches that are out for themselves -- this is just business, don't kid yourself. And you know the worst thing about it, even if it does somebody some good somewhere which
I can't possibly imagine, you'll never know the difference. You're just sweating and kidding yourself
- and you're kidding yourself if you think your new business partner is going to keep his hands off that girl -- or that she'll keep her hands off him.

LESTER
(he turns like a shot)
What are you talking about?

INT. BISTRO - LESTER AND FELICIA
FELICIA
(she laughs)
-- think what you have time to think, Lester.
Lester grabs her.

LESTER
What are you talking about,
Felicia?
Suddenly there's a rumble in the room and East has stopped chanting. Several men have stepped to the center of the room.
One of them in a slate suit raising both hands.

DET. YOUNGER
Excuse me, Senator. Ladies and gentlemen, we're going to have to evacuate this room as quietly and quickly as possible. There's nothing to worry about. We'd like you to exit through the door here on my left... down the steps into the street, please!
There are whisperings and rumblings of 'a bomb' and rejoinders to the effect that it's a hoax. Nevertheless the exodus begins and grows to bedlam. Waiters who had been

fawning over jeweled ladies are now unceremoniously pushing them down the stairs, even going over them to make the entrance.

OUTSIDE the emergency doesn't keep autograph hounds from inhibiting the exit as they try to hold up celebrities in the crowd that flows onto the street. Jill and Johnny Pope are caught up in the swirl of the crowd. Pope temporarily loses Jill. He looks around. Jill taps him on the shoulder.

JILL
-- here I am. Now what?
Pope turns.

POPE
Well -- as I see it we've got two choices. We can hang around here and wait for the bomb to go off, or we can go to my party.

JILL
Let's do that.
Lester is with some security people, trying to find out what they're doing.
B.G. are several police cars, a fire truck, and the fire truck ambulance. Lights are flashing.

LESTER
-- have they located it?
Somebody shrugs. A CAR HONKS. Lester is pulled to the side.

LESTER (CONT'D)
(looking toward driver)
-- oh, sorry.
Then he sees it's Felicia. She gives him the finger, and lays rubber nearly sideswiping him.

ONE OF THE SECURITY MEN
What was that all about?
Somebody else says 'who was that?' Lester shrugs.

INT. SAMMY'S HOUSE - GEORGE AND JACKIE are dancing to a tape of 'Good Vibrations.' George's coat is off, his tie loose. They are near the entryway and sitting on a large staircase b.g. a young girl can be SEEN breast feeding her baby.
George and Jackie are obviously enjoying themselves. The tape ends. George's silk shirt is clinging down the center of his back.
He moves with Jackie, where she picks up a coke at the bar.
A black in a caftan with a huge Afro offers Jackie a joint.
She takes a drags, she and George move outside the living room. As they walk she hands the joint to George who hands the joint to a couple of girls lying on a low couch by the door -- all without really losing stride.

OUTSIDE SAMMY'S - NIGHT
There's a long rolling lawn. The lights are soft coming from the living room, the MUSIC more muted. Jackie, nevertheless, is breathing rather heavily from the dancing. George is looking at her intently, too intently for her not to notice.
She appears not to notice.

GEORGE
What are you looking at?

JACKIE
The lawn -- it looks like it goes on forever, doesn't it?
She turns back to George.

GEORGE
-- yeah.

JACKIE
-- look, you don't have to entertain me...

GEORGE
(a slight laugh)
Am I entertaining you?

JACKIE
We're friends.

GEORGE
-- sure.

JACKIE
-- well, if you feel like playing, go play...
Jackie looks past George into the living room.

JACKIE (CONT'D)
-- there's a lot of players in there --
The TWINS come up behind George, and Jackie, grabbing George.
The move should be a little startling almost as if it were an attack.

TWIN ONE
George!

TWIN TWO
George!
They grab George and spin him around, temporarily pushing
Jackie OUT OF SHOT.

GEORGE
(pleasantly)
Hey, what's happening.

TWIN ONE
We're going to the jacuzzi.

TWIN TWO
Right now.

TWIN ONE
(tugging)
C'mon with us --

GEORGE
In the jacuzzi?

TWIN TWO
Sure, why not?

TWIN ONE
Come on, George --

GEORGE
No, later, maybe -- go ahead, I'll catch up with you --
(they head off)
I've got --
He turns back to Jackie to finish what he was going to say, and she's not there. Only a
wisp of her cigarette smoke hangs in the air, and then it disappears.
George looks surprised and disappointed.

INT. KITCHEN
Several tall stringy types are eating out of the refrigerator, with a couple of dogs eagerly
watching, others are eating hash cakes off the formica counter.
RED DOG sits in a corner, sipping wine out of a measuring cup. He smiles and looks
up to Jackie, who has her arm on his shoulder. Strobe lights from an adjacent room can
be SEEN

PERIODICALLY.
RED DOG
Where the fuck you been, Jackie?
London?

JACKIE
-- no.

RED DOG
Real good to see you, man.

INT. KITCHEN - JACKIE AND RED DOG
JACKIE
So what's been going on, Red Dog?

RED DOG
Hey, it's the same old shit, ain't it? No matter where you go, it's the same old shit.
Nothing ever changes, nothing, man, nothing.
(with sudden intensity)
Hey -- you ever been to Cuuliacaan?
George, a little hastily moves through the kitchen, spotting
Jackie. He's nearly upended by a couple, tall man and woman at the refrigerator. They
grab him and kiss him, and he shakes through them moving to Jackie.

GEORGE
-- where'd you go?

JACKIE
-- oh I thought you were --

GEORGE
-- what?

JACKIE
Nothing.

RED DOG
Hey, man, what's happening?

GEORGE
Nothing.

RED DOG
That's right, man!
And he laughs. George silently takes Jackie's hand and they move through the kitchen
and out of doors toward the grounds in the rear of the house.

EXT. BISTRO PARKING LOT - JOHNNY POPE
The crowd has thinned out to a trickle, but Pope's red
Porsche is hemmed in by the fire trucks and a couple of other cars.
Pope is vainly trying to talk to firemen and policemen to move their trucks and they
keep referring him to someone else.

JILL AND LESTER
Lester stands, swaying a little unsteadily in the lot. The
Deputy secret service man seen twice earlier, comes on up to
Lester.

DEPUTY
-- we can't find a thing, Mr.
Karpf.

LESTER
(turns to him)
Can't find what?

DEPUTY
No bomb.

LESTER
-- oh -- well that's good, isn't it?

DEPUTY
(he's scrious)
It's good if there's no bomb. If there is a bomb and we can't find it, that's not good.

EXT. BISTRO PARKING LOT
Lester thinks this over.

LESTER
No of course not.

POPE
(coming up to Jill)
-- we're going to be here all night.

JILL
-- why?

POPE
-- these bastards have me hemmed in.

LESTER
(to Jill)
-- what's the problem, honey?

JILL
-- his car. They have it blocked.

LESTER
Oh that's no problem.
(to Deputy)
-- take care of this boy's problem, will you, Gene?

DEPUTY
-- sure.
Pope and Deputy go off together.

LESTER
-- listen, I wonder if you kids could give me a ride? I'm kind of stranded here.

JILL
Sure thing, Mr. Karpf. C'mon.
They walk toward Pope's car. The trucks are being driven off.

LESTER
Everything okay, son?

POPE
Terrific. Now all I have to do is find my car keys.
He heads back into the Bistro. Lester and Jill stand outside the Porsche.

JILL
-- I'll get in the back --

LESTER
-- oh no, honey, I'll do that...

JILL
-- there's not much room --

LESTER
That's fine --
Lester opens the car door and pulls back the seat. He has a hell of a time squirming into the back, but tries to be lighthearted about it. Jill gets into the front.

INT. PORSCHE
The door on the driver's side is still open and Lester's feet are poked out it. His head is pushing on the canvas top.

LESTER
See, nothin' to it.
Jill turns and smiles, but it's a mistake since Lester's upper body is almost leaning on her as it is. Lester puts his hand behind Jill's head, forcing her to hold the position, almost nose to nose with Lester.

LESTER (CONT'D)
What did you say your name was, sweetheart?

JILL
Jill.

LESTER
(not moving his head)
Jill.
Jill can't really move her head back and Lester is obviously captivated by Jill's face.

JILL
(trying to be casual)
-- yes, Jill.

LESTER
(still holding her)
Gee... that's wonderful, Jill.

JILL
(very uncomfortable)
Thank you.

LESTER
(fondling her head, moving her closer)
-- just wonderful.

POPE is heading back to his car. He stops when he sees Lester's feet hanging out the door.

POPE (CONT'D)
(another irritant)
Oh, no shit.
Pope gets into the car.

POPE (CONT'D)
Hi, what are we doing?
Lester falls back and hits the isinglass rear window. Pope notices.

JILL
Oh, Johnny, Mr. Karpf needed a ride home and I said we'd take him. Do you mind?

POPE
(furious)
Of course not.

LESTER
Call me Les.

POPE
Where to, Les?

LESTER
Oh, say, how would you kids like to stop off for a drink?
Jill and Johnny Pope exchange glances. Jill shrugs to say, gee I'm sorry. Pope nods.

POPE
Well we'd love to, but we're going to another party.

LESTER
Well... that's wonderful -- I'll stop by there for a drink.
Pope is furious. He starts the car, backs it up quickly, jostling Lester around as he goes.
Lester chuckles.

EXT. FREEFORM SWIMMING POOL - JACKIE AND GEORGE - NIGHT lie
side by side on deck chairs at the end of the pool. The house and upper grounds are
obscured by neat rows of hedges and all sorts of random shrubbery. Jackie and George
watch the Twins splash and flounce around in the jacuzzi with a couple of androgenous
men. The Twins stand up in the jacuzzi, arm in arm and half move, half throw
themselves to another end of the jacuzzi.
Jackie smiles. She stretches, yawns.

JACKIE
(lazily)
-- very nice, very nice.

GEORGE
(yes)
-- mmm --
A pause. She glances at George scarcely moving her head.

JACKIE
-- but you never were much of a tit man --

GEORGE
Mmmm --

JACKIE
-- ass and legs --

GEORGE

Look who's talking.

JACKIE
Me?

GEORGE
-- yes, you --

JACKIE
Well of course. Who loves a big fanny on a man?

GEORGE
Not me, pal.
Jackie laughs. The Twins have gotten onto some sort of splashing contest with the boys.
Water hits George and
Jackie. They're hit again. They shrug, George rises, takes
Jackie's hand. They walk on around the pool, beside and along a maze of hedgerows.

EXT. SAMMY'S - THROUGH PORSCHE WINDOW as the slow moving car catches the rolling lawn seen earlier and the neat hedgerows which wind around the property.

LESTER
Whose place is this?

INT. SAMMY'S FOYER by the open staircase. Pope is greeting Sammy. Introducing Jill. Sammy's a tall, Jesus figure with an Indian shirt that goes to the knees on his levi's.

SAMMY
Sure I know Jill.
Lester is staring in some wonder at the girl who is still sitting on the staircase, nursing her baby. She looks up, smiles at Lester, who manages a nod back, doesn't take his eyes off the sight.

POPE
(noticing)
-- the bar's in there, Les.

LES
(embarrassed)
-- oh, fine.
He strolls off toward the bar which is half visible through the open foyer.

AT THE BAR where Jill and George were earlier. Lester's ordered a drink.
The huge black in the Afro offers him a toke. Lester stares at it dumbly.

LESTER
(a little lamely, indicating drink)
... I'm...
He takes his drink and half toasts the black. He stops and his eyes PAN the room. Lester is virtually the only person on his feet. Everyone else is either on the floor or on deep sofas, side by side, head to feet, barely talking, barely moving. In fact the most mobile thing in the room in smoke from the joints.

INT. LIVING ROOM - LESTER
Lester shakes his head as if to clear it. He takes a drink and almost on cue the ACID ROCK MUSIC HITS and the strobe lights go on.
Lester is momentarily alarmed, as if it had something to do with his drink. He manages to stagger out of the strobe light effect, hangs onto a railing in the next room.

INT. KITCHEN - JILL, RED DOG AND POPE
Jill stands over Red Dog who hasn't moved an inch, his measuring cup of wine still half filled.

JILL
-- so what's new, Red Dog?

RED DOG
Nothing, man. Same old shit. It's the same old shit wherever you go, nothing ever changes.
Pope looks up, sees Lester just outside the kitchen door.

POPE
Jill, scraves is a --
He points toward the kitchen door where Lester looks like he's about to enter.
Pope takes Jill and they move out the back door in the direction of the rear grounds that Jackie and George had taken earlier.

LESTER peers into the kitchen. It's filled mostly with unkempt beards. He decides against it, turns up a small staircase and continues up it until he finds himself in a den. Several people are seated on the floor, quietly smoking and watching television. They seem a shade better dressed than those in the kitchen.
Lester squints at the set which is a little blurry and partially blocked, by someone sitting directly in front of it. He kneels by a fortyish man in a bush jacket smoking a pipe.

LESTER
(whispering)
-- how's it going?

INT. DEN
MAN WITH PIPE
(quietly)

-- just fine.

LESTER
(squinting to see)
-- is that Illinois?

MAN WITH PIPE
(taking a good look at
Lester, then)
No, that's Sally.
Lester looks at the screen. Sally, handled by bare arms, is being placed on a foam rubber
cushion. She laughs.

LESTER
(dumbly)
-- Sally?

MAN WITH PIPE
(pointing with his pipe stem to a girl by
Lester's ear, also watching the set)
-- Sally.
Lester looks at Sally. She looks at Lester, nods. Turns back to screen to watch herself.
Lester turns from Sally to see a television camera and the foam rubber mattress, now
abandoned. Lester shakes his head.

OUTSIDE ON GROUNDS WITH JILL AND JOHNNY POPE
They're walking through shrubbery and hedges that lead them to a pair of empty deck
chairs by the jacuzzi end of the pool. One of the Twins is still in the jacuzzi.

JILL
-- so when are you going to Egypt?

POPE
You mean when are you going to
Egypt?
Jill laughs. She turns and shakes her finger at Pope.

JILL
Now I didn't mean that, you rat.

POPE
Two weeks from tomorrow.

JILL
You're going?

POPE
You're going.
Jill stops cold. She turns to Pope.

JILL
You're kidding.

POPE
Those Arabs won't be when they start chasing you around the sand dunes.

JILL
(laughing)
Johnny!
(she hugs him)
Why didn't you tell me before?

POPE
-- just before I ask you out? I can't do that. Let's get out of here before good old Les catches up with us again.
There's a flash of light from the poolhouse window. Jill turns toward it, then back to Pope, still making up her mind.
ANGLE SHIFTS SLIGHTLY to HOLD on light from window.

INT. POOLHOUSE - GEORGE AND JACKIE
George has pulled a pair of cokes out of the fridge. He's looking at Jackie, closes the refrigerator lamely. It opens again and he closes it again.

JACKIE
What's wrong?

GEORGE
-- do you want ice?
Interior poolhouse lit now by lights from outside.

JACKIE
-- no.
George pops the tops of the cans, hands one to Jackie.
Neither one of them drink. They're staring steadily at each other, their eyes shining from reflections from the tennis court lights which someone has turned on.

GEORGE
(finally)
-- we're kidding ourselves.

JACKIE
(staring right back)

-- we are?

GEORGE
-- last night I dreamt I was fifty years old and Mary told me I was supposed to meet Jill at the shop.
It seared me shitless.

JACKIE
Why?

GEORGE
I can't imagine being with Jill when she's fifty years old. I can't imagine not being with you.
George moves to her. Jackie is waiting for him. They kiss. It is long and lingering and deliberate. George breaks away and goes to the poolhouse door. There's no lock, only an eye latch on the screen door. He latches it, tests it. It gives slightly. Nevertheless he shuts the door and heads back to
Jackie who stands waiting.

JACKIE
-- but what about her? I don't want to hurt Jill.
George takes the coke out of her hand. She lets him.

LESTER walks back in the foyer, holding a drink, swaying. The strobe lights are going again in the living room.
Suddenly he sees a girl, at least half nude, her huge painted lavender tits flashing at him through the strobe lights. The vision disturbs him greatly.
He carefully steps down into the room in an effort to get near her. She seems to move. He moves after her through the lights down the length of the room, going as quickly as prudence allows. Finally when they reach the end of the living room she's disappeared. Then he looks out and sees her poised at the top of the steps a few yards away by the hedged path that leads down to the pool.
He lunges toward the vision, and bounces off a sliding glass door.

JILL AND JOHNNY POPE have made it through the entrance and Pope's Porsche is in sight. Jill suddenly stops and looks at Pope.

POPE
What's wrong?

JILL
We can't really leave that poor man here alone.

POPE
-- he'll never know the difference.
Jill is clearly thinking about something else besides Lester.

JILL
-- still -- at least we should tell him we're going. C'mon.

POPE
(going along with it, protesting)
I'm telling you he won't know the difference.

BY THE POOL - LESTER now with a sizable bump on his head he moves with the care that only tightrope walkers and drunks can move: every step is a possible disaster.

TWIN
(from Jacuzzi)
Hey.
Lester looks down, sees one of the Twins. Her arm is outstretched, her breasts dripping water VISIBLE through the shrubbery spotlights. She's holding a joint.

TWIN (CONT'D)
-- it's getting soggy.
Lester takes it.

THE GUY WITH HER
-- just put it on the bench over there and come on in.

LESTER
-- in there?

THE GUY
Sure.
Lester takes the joint and with fierce concentration makes it over to the bench. He puts the joint down.
Stares at it. He looks up and there's the other Twin standing beside him, nude, with her breasts visible through the towel loosely flung over her shoulders.

TWIN
(meaning joint)
Could I have that?
Lester silently hands it to her. Stares at the pool and the other Twin isn't there. He looks back and the one who had taken the joint is gone. He looks back to the pool and the other Twin surfaces with the force of Flipper, beside the Guy in the pool.
Lester stares, then he sighs and pulls off his pants, almost falling down as he does.
Carrying them, he walks over to the edge of the jacuzzi.

LESTER
Say --

THE GUY
-- what is it now, man?

LESTER
Do you know where I can find a towel?

THE GUY
-- the poolhouse.
Holding his trousers, his tux shirt hanging half down over his boxer shorts, Lester moves
on over to the poolhouse. He tries the door. The latch creaks. He pulls at it again and
the latch pops open. He starts to open the door, then hears the unmistakable sounds of
a couple in the throes of intense love making. The girl is quite carried away.
Lester hesitates. He listens as her sighs, interspersed with fetching little sobs begin to
mount in intensity. He thinks better of it. He takes his hand off the door knob and quietly
closes the screen door.
He starts to walk away, then notices the window on the side.
He can't resist. He moves to it. He can't see anything. He moves closer. The dim, dark
but classical outline of a man mounted on a woman moving with ease but increasing
intensity can be SEEN. Lester watches. The SOUNDS are not as loud from this angle,
but gradually they can be HEARD as the woman's cries grow louder. Lester is glued to
the window.

JILL'S VOICE
-- there you are. Les. Les -- Les --
Les, we're leaving.
The ANGLE has BROADENED to SHOW Lester holding his pants, not taking his face
away from the window. Jill and Johnny Pope stand beside him.

LESTER
Shhh --
(with genuine awe)
-- now that's what I call fucking.
Pope almost inadvertently tries to look in the window.
As he does, a light begins to flood the room. It is the refrigerator door slowly opening,
due in part to the rhythmic impact of the lovers transmitted through the sofa to an end
table to another end table and to the refrigerator.
It opens until the light shines on the upper body and face of
George and Jackie.

LESTER who has been smiling continues to smile until the enormity of the image hits
him. His face freezes. It is harsh and determined. He turns slowly away from the window
and walks past Jill without looking at her.

JILL
-- what --
She turns to the window and sees George and Jackie herself.

JILL (CONT'D)
(watching)
Oh my God. Oh no, oh no. Oh no.
She turns and picks up a wrought iron end table and hurls it through the window, shattering the glass everywhere.

JILL (CONT'D)
(screaming)
You son of a bitch! You bastard!

WITH GEORGE AND JACKIE
George has leapt up.

GEORGE
Honey? Where've you been? We've been looking everywhere for you.
Jackie doesn't move, only stares wide-eyed through the broken window at the screaming Jill.

JACKIE
(softly)
Oh God.
An ashtray is hurled into the room, smashing against the wall, and Jill can be SEEN now storming off with Pope.
George, with one leg in his pants, rushes over to a far window, pulls it open.

GEORGE
Jill! Jill! Jill, goddammit!
He's got the pants on backwards. He turns back to Jackie who has already slipped into her dress, is stuffing pantyhose into a purse.

GEORGE (CONT'D)
-- Jesus --

JACKIE
-- well you better go after her.
He bends down, turns his pants around, and is hopping into them.

GEORGE
-- shit...
(he grabs his shirt)
... wait here, honey --
He runs out of the door, beside the pool, past the jacuzzi and into the maze of hedgerows.
The Twins stand motionless side by side in the water.

TWIN ONE

George?
(to Twin Two)
Who was that?

TWIN TWO
Far out.
George, searching wildly through hedgerows, is calling Jill.
He can't find her. He finds himself next to a ten foot ivy covered wall. He can't reach the top. He moves along the wall... arrives at a wrought iron gate. It's locked. He peers through the gate calling frantically:

GEROGE
Jill, honey?
Inches from his face on the other side of the gate, the bare teeth of a huge German Sheperd GROWL at him viciously. George chooses to go up the hedgerows toward the living room of the house.
He trips and falls.

INT. LIVING ROOM
George running through the strobe-lit party to the foyer.
He's bare-footcd, but his pants are on. His frilly shirt is unbuttoned.

INT. FOYER - GEORGE breathing heavily, spots Red Dog.

GEORGE
Hey, Red Dog. You seen Jill?

RED DOG
She just went out the door, man.
George charges out the door in time to see the red Porsche's taillights blink bright at the end of the driveway before it purrs off into the night.
George turns and runs back into the house and through the strobe-lighting living room.

AT THE POOLHOUSE
George heaving deep breaths now runs on into the poolhouse.
The refrigerator door still hangs open. Window glass is scattered on the floor, and George steps on it, cutting his foot, hopping a little, pulling out a shard. Jackie's gone.

GEORGE
Jackie?
He opens the poolhouse bathroom door.

GEORGE (CONT'D)
Jackie?
He runs back out the door of the poolhouse.

EXT. POOLHOUSE
GEORGE
Jackie?

TWIN ONE
She went up to the house, George.

TWIN TWO
You're a trip and a half, man.

INT. THE HOUSE
George runs through the living room again and the strobe lights. Again he reaches the
foyer. Red Dog is still there.
George is heaving deeply now.

GEORGE
Hey... you seen... Jackie...

RED DOG
(pointing)
-- out the door, man.
GEORGE charges out the door, this time seeing Jackie's 230SL pulling away, tires
screeching.

GEORGE
(shouting)
Jackie!
He looks down defeated. His foot is bleeding on the pavement.

EXT. HIGH ROAD - NIGHT
George on his motorbike, COVERED by a few bars of Buffalo
Springfield's 'For What It's Worth,' has thrown on a peacoat but kept on his velvet
trousers. He's riding up what should now be a familiar road to Jill's. The lights from the
city below flash in and out of view.

JILL'S GARAGE - GEORGE pulls in. Her slot in the three car garage is empty, only
the oil slick stares at him.
There's the SOUND of a CAR coming down the road. He looks up expectantly. As it
comes by the morning newspaper is tossed at his feet.
George turns and fishes in the hanging planter by the door.
He pulls out a key, blows the dirt off it and goes inside.

INT. JILL'S - GEORGE - NIGHT
GEORGE
(swaying in)
Jill... Jill... Jill.

He looks in bedroom, then moves back to the phone and dials.
It rings three times.

OPERATOR'S VOICE
Jackie Shawn.

GEORGE
-- yeah, this is --

OPERATOR'S VOICE
-- yes, George.

GEORGE
I guess you haven't heard from her yet.

OPERATOR'S VOICE
Not yet.

GEORGE
Okay... thanks...
Hc hangs up. Stares around the room. Jill's apartment is, as usual, good-little-girl tidy.
(A contrast with Jackie's particularly kitchen.)
George walks over to the window and look's at the city. He walks out onto the deck and
sits in a deck chair.

DISSOLVE TO:
GRAY SCREEN
There is the SOUND of a CAR IDLING.
George opens his eyes. Above him is the carport and Jill's yellow Mustang has just
pulled in. George rises. He walks into the living room as Jill comes down the steps to
the kitchen, carrying the paper. The kitchen clock reads 4:44.
George glances at it. Then back at Jill. She looks at him, frightened but not moving. Her
hair is stringy and she's got no makeup on. There's a bruise on the inside of her upper
arm and a small one on her neck, and one on her left thigh all of which George will note
in the course of the scene.
George looks her up and down.

JILL
I don't want to fight, George.

GEORGE
I don't want to fight either.
Look... uh -- I love you.

JILL
Bullshit.

GEORGE
(moving to her, taking her arm)
I do, Jill.
At this point he notes the arm bruise. Jill stares back at him unflinching. George smiles.

GEORGE (CONT'D)
How come you took your own car?

JILL
(getting a cigarette)
I didn't want him meeting me here.

GEORGE
Well that's something.

JILL
What is.

GEORGE
You didn't plan on fucking him tonight.
Jill doesn't answer.
She walks into the bedroom, kicks off her shoes, starts to take off her dress, then changes her mind and puts on a robe over it.

GEORGE (CONT'D)
You did fuck him, didn't you?

JILL
I'm very tired, George.
Jill goes into the living room. George grabs her arm again.

GEORGE
Didn't you, baby?

JILL
Let go of me.
George doesn't.

JILL (CONT'D)
Let go of me or I'll scream, I'll call the police.

GEORGE
Oh, Christ.
He lets go of her. The PHONE RINGS. Jill answers it. Her tone alters appreciably.

JILL
Oh, hi... listen, can I call you back?... Yes... no, everything's fine, really... bye.
She hangs up.

GEORGE
That was him.

JILL
Yes.

GEORGE
You told him I was here and he wanted to know if I was beating you up.
Jill smiles thinly.

JILL
Yes.

GEORGE
Well, did you get a job out of it at least?

JILL
I'd like you to leave now.
George doesn't move. Jill goes over and fishes into a tote bag by the wall. She returns with Felicia's missing earring.

JILL (CONT'D)
-- and take this with you.

GEORGE
Where did this come from?

JILL
Who knows, I'm sure you don't -- but if it'll help any, I found it in your bed.
George nods. Jill's anger is growing and her hurt is beginning to surface now. Tears start welling in her eyes.

JILL (CONT'D)
(unsteadily)
So who else was there besides
Jackie? Huh?... huh?

GEORGE
Baby, don't do this. I do love you.

JILL
Obviously there were others, weren't there?

George stares at Jill. Then:

GEORGE
Obviously.

JILL
How many?

GEORGE
What do you wanna know for?

JILL
I just want to know, that's all.

GEORGE
What difference does it make?

JILL
I just want to know while we were seeing each other... I just don't want girls looking at me and knowing and me not knowing...
Jill is crying a little now and looks very vulnerable. George moves to her and tries to put his arms around her.

GEORGE
Baby, please don't... I love you.

JILL
(breaking away)
I don't want to be a fool!... I want to look them in the eye and say, I know!

GEORGE
(she's backing up, he's trying to touch her)
Baby, don't do this --

JILL
(fighting for control)
-- it'll help me if you'll tell me.

GEORGE
-- please, baby --

JILL
-- no, it'll help me, really --

GEORGE
How?

JILL
I'll know you've lied to me... all along. I'll know you're incapable of... love... that'll help me... not now, but eventually.
It's been rising in him the last few exchanges. Now all
George's restraints seem to leave him. He stops trying to touch her and stands his ground, exploding:

GEORGE
You dumb cunt, everybody fucks everybody, grow up, for Christ's sakes. You're an antique, you know that? Look around you -- all of
'em, all these chicks they're all fucking, they're getting their hair done so they can go and fuck, that's what it's all about. Come into the shop tomorrow and I'll show you -- I fucked her, and her, and her, and her, and her -- I fucked 'em all!... That's what I do, I fuck. That's why I went to beauty school, to fuck. I can't help that, they're there and I do their hair and sometimes I fuck
'em. I stick it in and I pull it out and that's a fuck, it's not a crime.
George leans on a glass topped coffee table for support, not even bothering to look at Jill. Jill has been pulled together a little more by the speech.

JILL
... well I'm glad you told me.

GEORGE
(his eyes closed)
Jesus.
His tone has indicated disbelief and disgust.

JILL
I am... I mean, you know, that's...
She can't finish It.

GEORGE
What? What? What? What? What?

JILL
... honest. At least you're honest with me.

GEORGE
Does it make you happy?
Jill doesn't answer.

JILL
I wish you'd go now.

GEORGE

That's all you've got to say?

JILL
-- yes.

GEORGE
-- tell me something -- did you talk about me?

JILL
George...

GEORGE
Did you?

JILL
Please!... that's not like you.

GEORGE
Yeah, I know. Did you?

JILL
George, now cut this out.

GEORGE
Did you?

JILL
Stop it.

GEORGE
Did you?

JILL
Yes, yes, I did.

GEORGE
What did you say?

JILL
George, if you keep this up I'm going to scream.

GEORGE
What did you say?

JILL
George...

GEORGE
What did you say?

JILL
I said you were a loser!
She starts to cry again. George smiles.

GEORGE
No, I'm not a loser, baby, I just sort of break even.
George turns and walks up the stairs and out the door.

EXT. GEORGE'S HOUSE
George shuffles up the steps to his front porch and into the living room.

INT. GEORGE'S LIVING ROOM
George finds himself facing Lester and two other MEN who look like hoods. Lester sits
in the chair George sat in the other night. Before him is a bottle of J & B, a paper bucket
filled with melting ice. The other men rise when George walks into the room.
Lester, glass in hand, stares silently at George.

LESTER
(to the other two)
Wait outside, would you?
The two Men walk toward George and pass him on either side, coming very close. Both
of them are much bigger than George.
They stare through George as they pass him.
George continues to stand there. Lester, drinking, continues to stare. Lester glances idly
around the living room. Then back to George.

LESTER (CONT'D)
You live like a pig.

GEORGE
Yeah.
(Lester doesn't answer)
How long have you been here?

LESTER
(looking it)
All night.

GEORGE
Well... who are those guys?

LESTER

What do they look like?...

GEORGE
Look, Lester... are you unhappy with me about something?

LESTER
Yeah, I'm unhappy with you about something.

GEORGE
Well, what?

LESTER
Godammit, George...

GEORGE
Now wait a minute...

LESTER
Sit down.

GEORGE
But...

LESTER
I said sit down!
One of the men opens the door and peers through the screen.

MAN
Everything all right?

LESTER
I'll call you, it's okay.
George site down. Lester has risen to his feet, a little unsteadily.

LESTER (CONT'D)
Now, George, I want to hear it from you. Either you admit it, man to man, to my face or I'll have him pound it out of you, and he does a hell of a job, believe me.
George nods.

GEORGE
I believe you...
Lester waits, standing over George.

LESTER
I wanna hear about it.

GEORGE
Oh Jesus Christ.
Lester slaps him.

LESTER
I wanna hear about it, George.

GEORGE
Hey, have 'em put me away, or whatever you're gonna do, okay?...
I'm too tired to lie, I'm too tired to tell the truth... I'm too tired for anything.

LESTER
I wanna hear about it.

GEORGE
What can I say!

LESTER
I wanna know your thinking, I wanna know how someone like you thinks.
Did you think you could get away with it, did you think you could put something over
on me? Does a guy like you get his kicks sneaking around behind people's backs and
taking advantage of them? Maybe that's your idea of being anti
Establishment!

GEORGE
I'm not anti-Establishment.

LESTER
That's got nothing to do with it...
You're so beyond my comprehension I can't even discuss it with you.

GEORGE
Then don't... just have 'em beat me up or whatever you're gonna do.

LESTER
No, not yet, not yet. You worry about it for a while, I've been worrying all night, now
you can worry.
A pause. Lester freshens his drink.

LESTER (CONT'D)
Was it me, did you have something against me?

GEORGE
What, do you think I planned it?

LESTER

Did they have something against me?

GEORGE
Didn't they tell you?

LESTER
I wanna hear it from you!

GEORGE
(agonized)
... how am I gonna tell you what they have against you?
I mean Jesus fucking Christ, they're women, aren't they? Have you ever listened to women talk, man? Have you? Well I do, I do 'til it's fucking coming out of my ears.
I'm on my feet all day, every fucking day, listening to women talk and you know what they talk about, don't you? Being fucked up by some guy. That's all that's on their minds.
I'm sure you've done something they could get pissed off about, what's that got to do with it? All women are pissed off, man, all of 'em. They fucking hate us!
Don't you know that?
Lester has listened to this with some alteration of his intensity.

LESTER
... yes, I follow your thinking on that.

GEORGE
We're always trying to fuck them... they know it and they like it and they don't like it... that's just how it is... look, it's got nothing to do with you, man. It just happened. Felicia's got nothing to do but shop and get her hair done and she knows she's getting older... her daughter hates her, what's she going to do, go to PTA meetings?

LESTER
Do you think Lorna hates her? I don't think she hates her. I mean she may resent her a little...

GEORGE
Oh, are you kidding, man? She hates her.

LESTER
Why, why do you think that is?

GEORGE
Oh, fuck, Lester, how should I know?

LESTER
Well, I don't know.
A pause. Lester goes to pour himself another drink.

LESTER (CONT'D)
(to George)
Want a drink?

GEORGE
No thanks.

LESTER
Have a drink.

GEORGE
Okay, thanks.
Lester gets up and goes to the kitchen.

LESTER
You don't have a clean glass in the house.

GEORGE
I know.

LESTER
(talking to himself)
I'll have to wash one out.
He turns on the faucet in the kitchen. He brings the glass.

LESTER (CONT'D)
Jesus, what a way to live. I never lived like this, not even when I was your age, not even when I never had a dime.
George takes the drink. Lester just shakes his head.

LESTER (CONT'D)
Hell of a way to treat a business partner, that's all I can say.

GEORGE
Who?

LESTER
Me!

GEORGE
Hey, you were never going to give me the money.

LESTER
(after a moment)
I was gonna give you the money.
Probably I was. Shit, I don't know,

I don't know anything anymore.
Lester sits and stares into his drink.

LESTER (CONT'D)
I tell you, you never know... you just never know... one minute you're here and the next... I mean a man at my age, how long have I got -- ten years? Five years? I wish I knew... what I was living for.
George looks at him.

LESTER (CONT'D)
... You can lose it all; you can lose it all no matter who you are... I don't know, what's the point of having it all. Look at me.
I don't have a goddam thing... the market's terrible right now, went down ten points last week, goddam
Lyndon Johnson!

GEORGE
Oh yeah...

LESTER
Yeah,, it goes up a little and then it goes down, maybe Nixon will do something. What's the difference, they're all a bunch of jerks. I wouldn't let 'em run my business, I can tell you that much. Not if I had any choice in the matter.
(after a moment)
I don't know what to do with you. I don't know, I don't know what's right or wrong anymore.

GEORGE
I don't either, Lester, I swear to you I don't.

LESTER
(suddenly)
What about Jackie?

GEORGE
What about her?

LESTER
I mean, how did that happen?

GEORGE
Lester, it just happened.

LESTER
She's nothing but a whore.

GEORGE
No --

LESTER
Just a whore, I go over there, have a few drinks and get my gun off.
I'm through with her, she's nothing but a whore.

GEORGE
No, man, no. You can say everybody's a whore. She's okay. I mean Jackie'll fuck around
but not that much. Somewhere she really likes you, Lester, and it's not just the bread.
She's okay.
Lester sits and thinks about that.

LESTER
You really think so?

GEORGE
Yes I do.

LESTER
I'm finishcd with her.
Lester goes to the door. He turns as if he'd just thought of something.

LESTER (CONT'D)
Oh, by the way, I think you oughta know -- Lorna thinks she's got the clap.

GEORGE
What?

LESTER
Yeah, the clap. That's what she thinks. But who knows -- I don't know.
George nods. Lester shakes his head.

LESTER (CONT'D)
I don't know anything anymore.
He opens the door and goes out. The two hoods are standing there. They look to Lester.

LESTER (CONT'D)
(to hoods)
Go easy on him, he's a nice boy.
George looks shocked. Lester laughs, gives George a playful punch.

LESTER (CONT'D)
Just having a little fun, George...
(to hoods)
Go on home.

(to George)
I'll call you later about the shop.
I'm beat. God, I'm beat.
With that, Lester's off.

EXT. SHOP - GEORGE - DAY pulls up. He goes into the shop.

INT. SHOP - NORMAN AND DEVRA
Norman is by the front desk.

NORMAN
You're late, George.

GEORGE
Devra, try Jackie Shawn will you?
And if you don't reach her, keep trying.

DEVRA
(on desk)
Mrs. Shumann and Mrs. Young are waiting. Mrs. Young is kind of p.o.'d.
George nods.

GEORGE
Where's Mary?

DEVRA
She hasn't showed up yet.

GEORGE
(grumbling something under his breath, then:)
Norman!
(to Devra)
Devra, I asked you to call Jackie.
Call her.

DEVRA
(perturbed)
All right.
Norman from upstairs shouts down.

NORMAN
What!

GEORGE
Somebody's going to have to wash
Mrs. Young. Mary's not here.

NORMAN
You do it.

GEORGE
(he's had about enough)
Look, Norman, I'm not the shampoo girl.

NORMAN
You are today.
George starts to say something but he's tired. He goes to his corner, slams his jacket down.

MRS. SHUMANN
Temper, temper, George.
George fiddles around with the shampoos and rinses, knocks over one where the top was not on, and the shampoo spills all over the table top and starts to drip on the floor.

GEORGE
Oh, Jesus, that fucking goddam Mary-
He starts to look for a rag and sees that Mary, wearing a cloth coat is coming into the shop.

GEORGE (CONT'D)
Mary! Get over here!
Mary moves very slowly, George waits, hands on hips. It should almost be a little faggy, his petulance as if, inevitably some of the shop must rub off on him.

GEORGE (CONT'D)
Mary, where were you yesterday?
Huh?
Mary doesn't answer.

GEORGE (CONT'D)
You ran out on me and you left it like a goddamn pig pen.
Mary's swaying.

GEORGE (CONT'D)
What's wrong, Mary, are you drunk?
Look, I've had a rough night, one of the roughest I've ever had, now
I'm not in the mood for any sulking bullshit, what's wrong? Are you sick? Are you drunk? Can you work?

MARY
Otis is dead.

GEORGE
-- Otis?
She points to his picture on the wall.

MARY
My son Otis. He was killed in
Vietnam. They done phoned me at the shop yesterday.
It's suddenly very quiet. The SOUND of the SHAMPOO DRIPPING on the floor can
be HEARD.

GEORGE AND MARY
GEORGE
Oh, Mary.
Mary starts to cry and like a little child buries her head on
George's shoulder.

MARY
-- you shouldn't talk to me like that no matter what, George... you know better...

GEORGE
-- oh -- sweetheart...

MARY
-- you shouldn't do me like that...

GEORGE
(hugging her)
-- please, please forgive me...

MARY
(crying)
-- you know better...

GEORGE
(after a moment)
-- why did you come in today?

MARY
-- left my bag, didn't have no money...

GEORGE
-- how did you get here?

MARY
-- took a bus.

GEORGE
-- c'mon, I'll get you home...

EXT. STREET - GEORGE - DAY on his cycle drives up Bowmont into Jackie's driveway. Her car is there.
George jumps off his bike, fairly races to the door. It's open and he barges in. He's met by Jackie's Yorkies who bark furiously, jumping up and down, nipping his pantlegs for attention.

JACKIE'S VOICE
-- just a minute, you're early --
Jackie comes walking out. She's carrying a large cooking spoon and wears an apron over a travelling outfit, a pantsuit. She's wearing more makeup than usual. She stops when she sees George.

GEORGE
-- good afternoon --

JACKIE
-- you've got to leave.
George is not prepared for this.

GEORGE
I've got to leave?

JACKIE
-- yes, honey, you've got to get out of here.

GEORGE
Why?

JACKIE
Lester's on his way.
George stares at her then walks past her into the living room. Bags are packed, a coat thrown over them. The wire kennel carrying cages for the Yorkies are beside the bags. George looks into the kitchen where Jackie's been cooking some pasta.

GEORGE
Where are you going?

JACKIE
Please, we'll have to talk later --

GEORGE
Look about last night --

JACKIE
(exasperated but not unkind)
Forget about last night, it's okay, we'll talk when I get back --

GEORGE
It's not okay, I mean we've got to talk now. Where are you going?

JACKIE
Look -- either you leave or I leave because I don't want the two of us here when Lester arrives. I just don't --
The level of her nervousness has just risen about fifty decibels. There's the SOUND of a CAR outside.

JACKIE (CONT'D)
My God that's him --
George looks out the window.

GEORGE
-- It's Malone's.

JACKIE
That's it, then I'm leaving.
With that she tosses the spoon onto an end table and rushes out the door. George starts after her. The DRY CLEANER comes to the door, stopping George.

CLEANER
Cleaners.
George has to fumble with Jackie's cleaning and keep the dogs contained. He does, tosses the cleaning down and races outside to his bike.

ON THE STREET he sees Jackie's car rounding the corner, going up the hill, winding around the curves. George guns his bike and takes off after her.

AROUND WINDING CURVES - GEORGE almost sideswipes a car parked on a hairpin turn. Jackie's on the curve above him.

AT THE NEXT CURVE - GEORGE catches up with her, pulls even to her.

GEORGE
Pull over, pull over!
He threatens to run her into the curb. She stops the car sharply and jumps out.

AT THE TOP OF THE DRIVE
They've reached a cul de sac where there's a parched 'view lot' not built on.
Yellow October weeds cover it and there's a huge television antenna in its center which sways slightly in an afternoon wind.

Jackie has run onto the lot, then slows to a walk. She grabs one of the rusty stays of the swaying antennas, stares down below her.
Her house can be seen from this angle, the Malone's truck just pulling away.
George comes up to her.

JACKIE
(looking below her)
You're going to kill me.

GEORGE
No --

JACKIE
(turning to him, imploring)
Well then what are you trying to do-

GEORGE
I want to marry you. I want to take care of you and I want your children, and I want you to be my girl. That's all I want. That's all
I want out of my life, and it's a lot.
She stares at him in disbelief. She actually clutches her stomach.

GEORGE (CONT'D)
Look, I don't know if I'll ever make it. I mean I'm a fuckup, but
I'll take care of you, I'll make you happy, I swear to God I will.
Jackie doesn't answer. She slowly sinks to the ground. George sinks beside her. Her eyes are wet.

GEORGE (CONT'D)
Jackie... Jackie?... answer me, for
God's sake, answer me.

JACKIE
If you knew how many times I wanted to hear you say that...

GEORGE
So I'm saying it...

JACKIE
It's too late...

GEORGE
What's too late about it? Look, we're not dead, are we? That's the only thing that's too late.

JACKIE

Lester's left Felicia. He's taking me to Acapulco on the five o'clock flight. He's asked me to marry him.

GEORGE
So what? You don't love him, do you? Answer me.

JACKIE
What's that supposed to mean?

GEORGE
I don't know... Jackie?

JACKIE
What?
George now is very near tears himself. What he says now he has to force out of himself, as if it's the biggest secret he holds.

GEORGE
I don't trust... anyone... but you...
George lets his head fall on her shoulder. She's kneeling, supported by the television aerial, and George cries quietly on her shoulder. She has her arm around him.

JACKIE
Oh my baby...
As she's holding George, and looking down the hill, Lester's silver Rolls pulls up. Lester gets out of the car, goes to the front door.

JACKIE (CONT'D)
God, there's Lester...

GEORGE
Don't go, Jackie...

JACKIE
I can't just let him stand by the door...

GEORGE
Don't leave me...

JACKIE
I've got to... I've got to tell him where I am.

GEORGE
What for?

JACKIE

I don't know -- I've got to.

She gets up and hurries over to her car, starts it and goes back down the hill. George sits under the television aerial and watches her car go down the hill, periodically flashing

INTO VIEW.

Finally she pulls up while Lester is pacing back and forth.

She hurries to him. He taxes her by the shoulders. They talk for a moment. The discussion looks like Jackie is giving Lester directions. She glances uneasily up toward George.

George is watching them.

He sees that Lester and Jackie have their backs to him, his arm around her shoulder, hers around his waist. They're going through the front door.

THE END